Handling Critical Moments with Grace

Toni Lynn Chinoy

Handling Critical Moments with Grace
Toni Lynn Chinoy
Copyright©2006

ISBN: 1-929910-12-6

Catapult Press
1564 Buck Mountain Road
Bentonville, VA 22610
540-636-4890

Acknowledgements

Every life journey includes crisis. I would like to thank my clients and friends who have shared so many of their stories with me. Through their experiences and their courageous experimentation with my sometimes counter instinctive advice, the concepts and principles in this text were tested again and again. Thanks go specifically to Susan Schmitt, who is the one of the bravest people I know. She is willing to take the risk on a new approach to old problems and her ability to look at her self honestly is wonderful. Others who particularly come to mind as courageous are Ingrid Lang, Geralyn Breig, Cathy Dussik, Mary Buhler, Kathleen Wilson-Thompson, David Evans, Carolyn Blesi, and Michael Krutza. They live their lives with honesty and integrity and serve as wonderful models of leadership.

Others who have made an impact on this work must also be mentioned. Tammy Savage and Lisa Maki, who believed in this work, and who backed that belief with their time and energy, deserve my gratitude. Terry Butler shared her expertise with grammar to help this work become more readable. Key to giving me the confidence to push forward with getting this book published was Janet Kelly. Beverly who is forced to work daily with someone who analyzes *everything* to the point of nausea (so says Cathy Dussik) deserves a medal

And lastly, I would like to give my special thanks to John Ahearn, for his creativity and persistence in helping to create the look to fit the content. His photography and his teamwork in creating the cover, along with his wonderful attention to detail, made what are often tedious processes, fun!

Wherever a man may happen to turn, whatever a man may undertake, he will always end up by returning to the path which nature has marked out for him.

~~~Goethe

Dedication

While in the process of developing this book, I had the opportunity to observe an astonishing example of handling a crisis with Grace. I dedicate this work to Ed Evans. His response to a life threatening illness was an inspiration to everyone around him. He exemplified the principles in this book and I am grateful to have been a part of this strong and resilient person's life.

Foreword

From the most sophisticated business negotiation to the simple daily interactions that make up our lives, there are significant moments which have the potential to change our future. There are patterns to our responses which may enhance or diminish our return on those moments.

Spin your wheels in anger, sadness, and despair or choose to use what is in front of you as a lever to lift yourself above it all. Assume that the symptoms of your discomfort are signals to send you searching for a better way.

Look into the eyes of your enemy and pretend he is your friend. Pretend that he is here to help you see yourself and the errors you make. Imagine a different purpose for his path crossing yours. Perhaps he really is not here just to torment you.

This text is about choice. It is also about learning skills and gaining understanding that can help you to create different outcomes. Learn to move beyond the instinctive responses that leave you angrier, sadder, or more embattled.

We all face obstacles. We have fears that constrict our thinking and our behaviors. Imagine the difference in your life and the lives of others around you if you challenged yourself only to make decisions which reflect Grace.

T.L.C.

Contents

The Foundation

Practice Applications

Confidence

Clarity

Trust

Appendix

The Foundation

Chapter I

Practicing Grace

Grace is a word with multiple meanings. For our purposes, they all apply. Grace can be a sense of effortless flow, beauty, generosity, mercy, or elegance. It can be a charming manner. Grace is a description of how you can interact in the world; it signifies a form of higher plane behavior that is rarely attainable with consistency.

The process of attaining Grace is an evolution. Like the most elusive fantasy, you have a moment when you think you have it. Suddenly you lose your balance over something that even you can see is silly.

The enemy of Grace is fear. Even the most controlled and cool-headed executive in the most complicated of deals may be operating from fear. As he or she moves through the sequence of steps, the only evidence of that person's lack of Grace may be in the result. The fears may be subtle, even subliminal, but the outcomes, to the trained observer, will often betray the hidden fears.

Responding optimally to the daily interference in our desires or dreams by others or by events requires practice; a lot of practice. Your responses to daily threats builds a skill set which permits you to interact in an easy, flowing manner in all situations.

If these skills are performed frequently and thoughtfully, your ability to manage the tougher, more significant events in a flowing manner is enhanced. If you do not challenge yourself to a high standard of response on a daily basis, it is less likely that you will perform ideally in real crisis.

To achieve Grace, one must be prepared to let go of control and refrain from overplaying the hand which has been dealt. For most individuals, this is the most challenging discipline to develop. Like the well-trained quarterback who knows exactly how long to hold on to the ball to enhance the odds of success, we need to learn the timing and strategy of achieving a long-term result. We must be able to do so even when we are watching the freight train rushing toward us.

The Three Fundamentals

In order to learn the practice of Grace, we must break it into manageable components.

There are three fundamentals vital to interacting with Grace. It is these three fundamentals which help you to elude the repetitive cycle of fear. They are often elusive in the height of battle. Mastery of the three fundamentals requires conditioning. The three essentials are Confidence, Clarity, and Trust. Imagine a Venn diagram with three circles labeled Confidence, Clarity and Trust. Assume that to execute with Grace you must operate within the intersection of the three circles. The greater the stakes, the more difficult it is to find that optimal balance of (A) Confidence, (B) Clarity and (C) Trust.

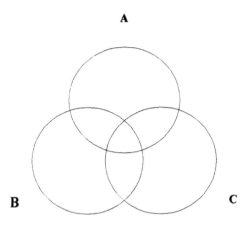

A

B   C

While knowing the fundamentals helps you to know where to focus, it certainly does not guarantee you an easy journey. There are specific, optimizing responses that support and reflect each of the fundamentals. If executed appropriately, these responses produce Grace. *Whenever you get stuck in fear, the optimal responses have the power to pull you out.*

The optimizing response in support of **Confidence** is *Flexibility*. Do you have the elegance to remain flexible even when you have decided that you absolutely must have your way? Acting with flexibility during the intense moments of life reflects total confidence in one's capacity to work with whatever the cards are offering. Rigidity is symptomatic of a lack of confidence.

Unfortunately for your ego, if you are not flexible, most intelligent people will believe that you do not feel confident. Instead, you send the message that you are fearful and need to control.

The optimal response in support of **Clarity** is *Curiosity*. Clarity is the ability, *in the moment*, to identify what is happening and why it is happening. When interactions become stuck or hostile, participants are often unaware of why. They frequently attempt to force their agenda without understanding the reason why what they want isn't happening.

The only appropriate response when things do not go your way is to become curious. For example, do you know why the outcome you desire *needs* to take place? Have you become so invested in the win that you have forgotten? Do you really know why you are getting resistance? Did you ask, or did you just assume? Are you assuming the motives of others when you could be *wrong*?

The optimizing response in support of **Trust** is *Detachment* which can be defined as the *absence of bias or prejudice*. Can you step back and see the natural order of things? Do you see that, over time, circumstances tend to right themselves and fall into patterns which actually make sense for the greater whole? Can you let go of righteousness long enough to allow the natural consequences of your (and others') choices to manifest? Can you eliminate fear and replace it with a trust in a greater power than yourself (as opposed to believing that you are all powerful)? Anger, fear, and sometimes even enthusiasm are the enemy of Grace.

Can you walk away when the outcome begins to lose its luster? Do you know when the Universe is telling you that this "deal" really should not occur? Perhaps it really is not in your own best interests to win. Do you know when to "fold 'em", or do you simply ignore all of the signs because you have become obsessed with winning?

You do not have to be religious to exercise trust in the natural order of things. You *do* have to be humble and you also need to pay attention to how things unfold around you. You must be prepared to accept that there is an order and rhythm to life. If you only believe in chaos, you will create unnecessary chaos for yourself and others.

It is important that you not misunderstand Trust. This text is not suggesting that you trust in others who are not trustworthy. That would be naive. Trust is the ability to trust both in yourself and in a larger force affecting you, your destiny and the destinies of others. This kind of trust calls for a more watchful and thoughtful analysis of what you see. It is dependent on your ability to clearly understand the law of cause and effect in the circumstances of your life.

Mastery of these three fundamentals (Grace) is achieved when you remain flexible, curious, and detached from bias in *all* moments. When you master this your results will begin to reflect your wisdom. You cannot fake Grace and you cannot turn it on like a faucet when you want to work your will. That is simply manipulation, which takes very little skill.

Things to Remember:

1. **When you are in an important moment and it isn't feeling right, do not attempt to force anything. Imagine that doing so is like trying to overpower a small knob on a piece of sensitive equipment. It might break. Slow down and study what is happening. Your feelings are telling you that you need more clarity.**

2. **If a situation you thought was resolved keeps coming back to you as unfinished, it probably means that the resolution of the situation is unfinished. You may have chosen the wrong path, forced a solution that is not viable, or attempted to avoid making a decision that you need to make. If you continue to attempt to recreate the same outcome, you will continue to get the same result. A confident person tries new things and considers other outcomes.**

3. **When things are not going as you hoped, assume that they are going exactly as they should. Explore other opportunities. A trusting person knows that there are always good reasons for adversity and obstacles.**

Chapter II

Know Yourself

The First Step to Enlightenment

Assume that the first step to easier, more flowing outcomes in your life is to understand and manage your fears. Grace starts, as does mastery of all things, with self-knowledge.

Are you self aware enough to recognize the moments and situations when you are insecure?

You must pay close attention to how you feel. Be alert for all symptoms of a fall from Grace (falling out of that easy, effortless flow). As you become more aware of your symptoms, you will attack your fears and obstacles more skillfully. Problems will be solved before they become BIG problems and life will take on a different quality; one you may have only imagined before you started the journey.

Recognize the Symptoms

Grace is your journey and it belongs to you alone. Your challenges and triggers will be unique to you. Your weaknesses are only yours. The symptoms of moving away from Grace, however, are relatively universal. Elements in both your own responses and those of others will demonstrate to you that you have moved away from Grace.

1. **Emotional Symptoms**: Any strong, negative emotion indicates a distance from your ability to behave with Grace. The most obvious destructive emotion is anger. If you are angry you have lost your focus. If you think of Grace as operating at your highest potential, you can see that you are no longer operating at your highest potential if you are angry.

    Note: If you doubt this, stand with your strongest arm outstretched and have someone push down as hard as they can while you resist.

Then, think about something that makes you angry and repeat the exercise. You will find that your arm is dramatically weaker when holding the emotion of anger. Anger and other strong emotions take away your ability to remain focused.

Excitement and enthusiasm can also cloud your judgment and be symptoms of a lack of objectivity. Your highest potential is again compromised. Your over-enthusiastic attachment to the outcome can cause you to get out of sync with the optimal flow. Emotions of any intensity are a way of flagging for yourself that you have lost neutrality.

Sadness is another symptom. Sadness is frequently a reflection that you have become caught in the past. If so, do your homework to find what you are still hanging onto. Find a way to let it go and move on. Easy to say...

2. **Physical Symptoms**: Physical symptoms are often the first clue that you have stepped away from the most ideal path. For example, long before you are consciously aware that you are losing your objectivity, you may start feeling a muscular tightness in whatever part of your body you tend to hold tension. Grinding of teeth, anxiety attacks, sleeplessness, may all be symptoms of a hidden, or maybe obvious, problem affecting your ability to achieve your desire in an effortless and flowing manner.

3. **Behavioral Symptoms:** Think of how you behave when you feel confident and relaxed. Are you behaving in a relaxed, non-obsessive way around this particular circumstance? If not, do you know why? Do you know what you fear? If you are not behaving in a way that you like, you will want to understand why and deal with it. Until you do, the fear will control your responses.

Behavioral symptoms of a lack of Grace include those moments when you attempt to control what is happening without sensitivity to the results. For example if you are clear that someone is attempting to undermine you, encroach on your turf, or make themselves look good at your expense, you are very likely to slip into "control mode". If you find yourself trying to undermine the other person, take away what he or she is trying to gain, close them out, or engage in any behavior that is not easy and flowing, you are probably in trouble. The outcome *will* reflect the input. You will often find yourself chastised or losing ground in spite of the fact that the other person is wrong and you did not initiate the situation.

Know Your Behaviors

The following chart includes many behaviors which indicate the person is acting from fear. You will also see a list of possible causes. This list is included to help you identify some of the patterns you fall into when you are uncomfortable or afraid. Later chapters will *begin* the process of identifying ways to overcome the instinctive responses indicated here.

Behavior	Possible Causes	Result/Outcome
Arrogance.	• Fear of being restrained, influenced, or controlled by something or someone else. • Inability to understand worth and roles of others. • Lack of flexibility in seeing value of multiple paths. • Inability to balance importance of relationships with getting results.	• Rejection, resistance and/or diminished self-esteem among those you must count on for results. This can exacerbate your sense of superiority and fear of dependency. • Loss of respect from those you treat disrespectfully. Others behave passive-aggressively to undermine your sense of power.

Behavior	Possible Causes	Result/Outcome
Approval Seeking.	• Low self-confidence, dependence on others. • Lack of clarity regarding worth of others.	• Loss of trust among those who believe you will sell them out to gain approval. • Misplaced loyalty to those who do not deserve it.
Neediness	• Fear of betrayal or rejection. • Lack of understanding of personal strengths and weaknesses.	• Attachment to controlling personalities. • Loss of freedom of thought and action. • Frequent sense of loss and betrayal. • Lack of self determination, victimization.
Judgmental/highly critical of others.	• Fear of personal failure. • Perfectionism. • Inability to detach from the actions and choices of others. • Lack of confidence.	• Lack of compassion for others. • Lack of personal tolerance for failure. • Constant fear of mistakes. • Highly controlling behaviors. • Conflict.

Behavior	Possible Causes	Result/Outcome
Controlling.	• Fear of unknown. • Lack of confidence in ability to handle surprises. • Fear of failure.	• Resistance and escape by others. • Constant state of personal anger. • Frequent sense of betrayal when others attempt to regain control.
Stubborn.	• Fear of instability. • Lack of imagination and playful curiosity.	• Rigidity. • Missed opportunities. • Lack of growth. • Stagnation.
Victimization.	• Inability to take responsibility for bad choices.	• Loss of control. • Manipulation by others. • Loss of respect.
Worry.	• Lack of trust in greater order.	• Needless anxiety. • Muddled thinking. • Stressful existence. • Chaos. • Missed opportunities.
Avoiding.	• Fear of conflict. • Low skill levels. • Lazy.	• Escalation. • Hostility. • Loss of control. • Loss.
Passive-Aggressive.	• Feeling of powerlessness. • Fear. • Sense of no alternatives.	• Mistrust. • Hostility. • Dislike. • Retaliation. • Increased bullying by others who are more direct.

Behavior	Possible Causes	Result/Outcome
Righteous.	• Sense of responsibility for the moral behavior of others. • Insecurity. • Judgmental. Perfectionism.	• Resentment. • Hostility. • Isolation. • Poor relationships.
Aggression/Bullying.	• Sense of powerlessness. • Lack of trust in outcome. • Habit (spoiled behavior).	• Creates fear in others. • Lack of honesty from others. • Missed information. • Sabotage.

Symptoms only tell you when you have encountered an obstacle to Grace. They do not tell you what it is or how to move around it. Before outlining key steps to more optimal behavior, there is one more step to knowing yourself. It may help you identify and avoid behaviors that take you away from Grace.

Know Your Patterns

There are repeating patterns which cause an individual to become emotional or less focused. These patterns often cause the destructive behaviors listed above. If you can identify the patterns particular or peculiar to your personal negative responses, and give them a name, your ability to manage your reactions and achieve Grace will improve.

Think of your unique patterns as a role that you play when others trigger your flawed self-confidence or your 'out of reach' trust in a benevolent Universe. For example, do certain personality traits cause you to turn into a "caretaker" at your own expense? Do you become a "crusader" or righteous when others let you down?

Recognizing your own response as a negative pattern is sometimes a challenge. You may even think of your reaction as a positive and powerful statement of who you are.

Unfortunately, if your response creates a reaction which causes others to resist you or makes your objectives more elusive, you are creating potentially unhappy, un-Graceful moments for yourself. Instead, if you can name the role that brings instant recognition and acceptance of your personal responsibility in creating a critical moment, you will work through the moment more quickly and with greater elegance.

Roles you play can also be related to the behaviors and choices of others. For example, if you have a pronounced sense of fairness, you will react negatively to people who do not treat others fairly or to any sense that you yourself are being treated unfairly. Looking back over your history you will see this pattern repeating itself throughout your life.

You may have a strong work ethic and respond negatively to those who take advantage of their employers. Perhaps illogical, emotional people tip you over the edge. Neediness from others can also trigger a negative response from you.

All of the above may occur to you as something that would upset most rational, stable people. However, when you have an issue that affects you at a *deep* emotional level it can cause more than normal distaste for the behavior or situation. This type of issue has the ability to turn you into an angry and judgmental person, taking you out of a state of Grace. This becomes your loss, not the other person's. Your objective is to overcome and rise above *all* triggers to which you have an intense emotional reaction.

It is rational to dislike negative behavior from others. Being taken advantage of, being used, being disliked, being misunderstood, being treated disrespectfully, etc., are all naturally offensive treatments. People of Grace can dislike these behaviors and remove themselves from others' ability to affect them, while still avoiding the emotional trap of fear and anger. You will find that your issues will manifest repeatedly until they are no longer issues. Unfortunately, the less conscious you are of the issue as a personal issue, the more painful the process will be.

27

With any pattern that triggers a strong emotional response from you, there is often a subtlety imbedded in the behavior which complicates your understanding. For example, fear of being taken advantage of is often accompanied by a strong sense of care-taking. You will step into a caretaker role without thinking and then resent it when others take advantage of your giving nature.

Your job is to identify *your* weakness that *allows* others to act in a way that angers you. You are going to identify what it is about you which attracts the behaviors you dislike.

For your own enlightenment, you might want to identify the pattern and then do the work of identifying what you do that repeatedly brings this pattern back to you. Your intense anger is often at yourself for once again allowing yourself to be set up.

Behaviors that trigger your anger:	Possible weakness it reveals in you:
Over-emotional/needy.	Fear of showing your own emotions or needs.
Poor work ethic.	• Perhaps you need to take over and be the hero when others do not perform. Their poor performance gives you room to prove how valuable you are. • You like to play the martyr. • You draw these people to you because they know that you will step in and take over.

Behaviors that trigger your anger:	Possible weakness it reveals in you:
Disrespectful.	• Inability on your part to command respect naturally. • Lack of personal self-confidence.
Being used.	Inability on your part to set appropriate boundaries.
Taken advantage of.	Caretaker personality; your ego may need to be recognized as a care-giver and you are not careful about how you apply it.
Lack of integrity in others.	Letting others repeatedly abuse you; going back for more after you know they lack integrity.
Unfair.	• Inappropriate expectations regarding what is "due" you without objective evaluation of what you have earned. For example, comparing raises or promotions with others instead of determining when you are really ready for what you are asking. • Not hearing feedback.

Things to Remember:

1.   When it does not feel right, it isn't.

2.   Pay attention to what it is that consistently gets your attention in

29

a negative way. For whatever reason, that is a weak spot in your quest for Grace.

3.   When you identify what you dislike, see if you can identify your own behavior that draws those individuals or circumstances to you.

4.   You will know your own critical moments (moment where you determine the flow of your life) by how you feel. Ignore them at your own risk. Over time, the issues around a specific critical moment, if ignored, will tend to increase in intensity.

5.   Try to be clear about your own patterns during critical moments. If possible, name them and use the name to remind yourself that you have lost control of your path. (Examples: doormat, overachiever, bully, etc)

6.   You are the creator of your reality. When in doubt, look within.

Chapter III

The Five-steps of the Cycle

If you can think of "life" as the physical, mental and spiritual experiences that constitute a person's existence, then think of your engagement and participation in life as an endless cycle (or loop) of five interlocking steps. If you are aware and knowledgeable about the steps and how they work, you can increase your effectiveness (Grace) dramatically.

There are opportunities in each of the five-steps of the cycle to choose Grace over fear and thereby redirect the flow toward a more optimal outcome.

Unless you understand and identify the step or level that you're in—both in the macro of your life's journey and the micro of the moment—you will miss significant opportunities to create more flow and beauty in your choices.

The ability to interact and engage with life effectively (i.e. with Grace) could be called an advanced form of human intelligence.

Human intelligence has many labels within the field of psychology including Moral Intelligence, Social Intelligence, Emotional and Interpersonal Intelligence. Simplified, intelligence can be considered one's ability to effectively integrate three forms of thinking: analytical, creative and practical.

The purpose of this text is to help you understand what the five steps are, and to improve your ability to think analytically, creatively and practically as you move through those five-steps. By improving your ability to think analytically, creatively and practically, you will become more effective at finding and eliminating the blocks to your Trust, Clarity and Confidence.

With practice, slowing down and finding Grace within the five-steps becomes a natural alternative to living with struggle and conflict.

Cycle of Repeating Steps

The steps, which are part of every single minute of your life and the life of everyone you know, are, in order:

Step 1: Critical Moment
The word critical can be defined as "of or relating to a condition causing an abrupt change in a quality, property or phenomenon." For our purposes, the phenomenon is your life. Critical moments are those key moments within which your actions have the potential to affect the direction or quality of your life (in a large or small way). Advanced students of Grace understand that *any* given moment has the potential to adjust and change the direction of their lives, making all moments critical moments.

Most of us, unfortunately, will be unaware of the criticality of a moment unless we are able to describe it as a problem or issue.

Step 2: Vision
In *every single instant* of your life, whether you are aware of it or not, you are in the process of creating your vision of what will happen next. If vision is "the way in which one sees or conceives of something", this part of the cycle suggests that you have choice in terms of how you do so. Are you making your choices thoughtfully or is it happening in the background of your mental processes?

When you identify and define a critical moment, your next step is to address the fact that all is not in flow and create a vision for the desired outcome. Make sure your visioning process does not focus on the worst that can happen. If you inadvertently use this crucial step of the process to validate your worst imaginings you may bring them about. Visioning is a very important aspect to creating flow in your life.

Step 3: Assessment
The assessment step is the process of consciously, or unconsciously, determining risk. There is an obvious data gathering element to this step. How do you determine risk effectively if you are operating from insufficient

data? If you are extremely good at this particular step, your life will reflect that proficiency. You will know when to take risks and also when not to.

Unfortunately many people are relatively unbalanced in their ability to perceive risk. Some, if not most, people are good at determining the cost of moving forward on a particular thought, initiative or action. They feel and fear the risks of action. However, determining the cost of standing still is under-appreciated. Many individuals become immobilized due to their fear of taking action, but fail to consider the potentially worse consequences of failing to act.

Step 4: Engagement
Engagement is the step in the cycle in which you make decisions, singly or in participation with others. Dialogue with others is considered engagement, but so too is the inner debate which causes a decision to be made when no one else is involved.

Engagement *should* feel effortless and flowing. If it feels confusing, frustrating, or frightening, then you or others are attempting to force an issue. It is possible you need to back up to steps I and II and revisit your conclusions.

Step 5: Execution
In this step decisions are carried into action and agreements have all been reached, whether internally or externally. During this step you will often see the flaws in your performance of steps 1, 2, or 3 in terms of cause and effect. If resources do not change hands, if people do not cooperate with their agreements, if sabotage occurs or if you are haunted by a sense of having made a mistake it is probable that the outcome was either forced or not clearly understood.

Keep in mind that the five-steps of the cycle are an endless loop. They continuously repeat themselves both in the larger context of your life and also in the specific problem you are addressing at the moment. You will find yourself performing in a play which is also part of a larger play, and so on and so on.

In this moment, and in every moment, you are typically involved in the five-step process, probably at multiple levels. You may be in step 2 (vision) on a specific problem, step 4 (execution) on a family project, and in step 1 (critical moment) in your life's journey. Within each step in the cycle, you must choose whether you will operate from Grace or from fear.

The more advanced you become in your understanding of the steps and their importance to your outcomes, the more skilled you will become at identifying the blocks to your best and most satisfying results. Your choice is to either be funneled through the cycle blindly and ignorantly, repeating past mistakes and causing yourself and others unnecessary grief, or to integrate the three fundamentals of Grace into each decision you make.

Think of the term in computer programming called a "do loop". (A do loop is any cycle of steps where, once entered, the sequence continually repeats itself with no escape.)When you are immersed in the five-steps with no awareness of your ability to manage and control your responses, you will essentially be caught in an endless do loop of fear-based reactions to whatever is occurring. Moving from a fear-based do loop to a cycle of Grace is achieved by understanding what is happening (clarity) and finding the confidence in yourself to stop repeating the old behavior. The next chapter will help you to recognize whether you are functioning at a level of Grace. The following chapters will help you to determine what to do if you are not.

Things to remember:

1. All moments of every day are made up of one or all of the five-steps of the cycle. The steps are manifesting at multiple levels in your life at all times.
2. Your awareness of where you are, where you should be, and how to respond to the steps of the cycle to achieve optimal results is key to changing the quality of your life.
3. Negative emotional, physical or behavioral responses to any situation indicate a potentially critical moment, which includes the opportunity to redirect your experience.

4. Knowing exactly which step you are on during any interaction is important to identifying appropriate responses. If things are not feeling right, your assessment of which step you are on may be incorrect or you may need to return to a previous step for reevaluation before continuing. For example, if you are clearly in the engagement step (decision-making) and it is going badly, your correction may be in realizing that you have inaccurately assessed the different risks (assessment). Or, you may need to develop a more appropriate (Graceful) vision of what *should* happen. In other words, work back up the cycle to find where you set up the current difficulties.
5. Each and every step offers a choice between fear and Grace with the difference in outcome being one of an endless repetitive cycle of fear, or a moment (or more) of effortless flow.

Chapter IV

Using the Five-Steps of the Cycle Effectively

Grace is a form of mastering Life. Naturally there are higher and higher levels of understanding and performance. We will start with a simple example so you can absorb the concepts before applying them to issues which are complicating your own life.

Suppose that you know by the way you feel that you are in a critical moment. You are angry, upset, tense, or hurt by something that is happening. These feelings are automatic warnings that you are within a critical moment which may affect the quality of your life.

If your personal symptoms are telling you that you are not operating from your highest potential in this critical moment, how do you adjust so the process feels as it should and the result begins to optimize?

The pathway to Grace is always through understanding the cycle of steps and how to integrate the three fundamentals of Grace into that knowledge. When you experience symptoms that indicate all is not as it should be, the starting place is always the first step of the cycle. In the following section we'll use a case study to walk you through the process of the five-steps of the cycle.

Case Study: A "Childlike" Example of Negotiating the Cycle

Obstacles to your achievement of Grace begin early with lessons learned in childhood. This first case study portrays how easy it is to start down the path of fear-based responses and how the impact of every journey can affect the quality of life in your future. This example will also illustrate the complexity of unraveling your responses as an adult.

Situation: A five-year-old and his mother are having an intense discussion regarding toys. She is determined that her son give away some of his toys. They have accumulated to the point that space is a major issue. The five-year-old is having a very emotional reaction to the potential loss of any toy.

The five-year-old is experiencing a critical moment that has the capacity to change the direction of his life. Overstated? Possibly it is. However, to him, it *feels* like one of the more intense moments of his life.

The optimal response represents the understandings and responses that might be arrived at if given a fair degree of Trust, Clarity, and Confidence (Grace). The sub-optimal response indicates the potential outcomes of a fear-based response without the benefit of the three fundamentals of Grace.

Note: the following example offers suggested responses for the individuals involved and their situation. There will always be different and/or better optimal responses than those described here depending on what fits best for you and your situation. Because every person has a different foundation, the goal is to seek *knowledge* and *wisdom* rather than the exact right answer. There is no formula to Grace, only process. Following this example, you will be given more information on what can go wrong, and what you can do about it.

Step 1: Critical Moment

1.   **Optimal response: Identification of this as a critical moment by the parent in response to the extreme fear being expressed by the child. Begin to define the fear. What is it?**

   a.   **The five-year-old is expressing a fear of not having enough. This fear is often identified as "scarcity". He is in the process of exploring a fear that he may carry with him into his adult life.**

   b.   **The underlying fear is loss of control.**

2.   **Sub-optimal response: The parent fails to recognize this as a critical moment for the child and the moment passes with the parent controlling the outcome and thereby exacerbating the sense of loss and scarcity, as well as the child's ongoing fear of loss of control.**

Step 2: Vision

1. Optimal Response: Instead of asserting control, the parent helps the child understand the pleasure of giving, perhaps by creating a vision of a child with no toys and how much one of his toys might mean to a child in that situation. This helps the child learn to create a sense of pleasurable and positive outcome from what was a very intense and fear provoking moment.

2. Sub-optimal response: There is no intervention in the child's thoughts or vision of not enough toys. Therefore, the tape playing in the child's head is one of losing something valuable. With no intervention, the default vision is the most negative version of what could happen.

Step 3: Assessment

1. Optimal Response: The parent helps the child take another look at the risks involved in giving away his toys. First, the parent works with the child to identify how real it is that he wouldn't have enough toys or that there will never be any toys to replace the ones that are given away. Then the parent helps the child look at potential issues involved in keeping the toys (for example, not having enough room for new toys). While all this may seem a bit trivial, please keep in mind the adult version of these same fears and how they can cripple a person's will to let go of things, jobs or people in his or her life at critical moments.

2. Sub-optimal Response: Again the parent does not understand the criticality of the moment and the child continues to fear that if he gives away the toys there will not be enough for him. Thus, his fear sways the decisions that must be made (to keep them or to let them go) without adding clarity, confidence or trust into the assessment process.

Step 4: Engagement

1.   Optimal Response: The parent and the child together agree
     that some of his toys are not played with as frequently and
     that perhaps he has outgrown them. Together, they create
     a pile of toys that are to be given away.
2.   Sub-optimal Response: Either the parent arbitrarily decides
     what to purge and asserts authority over the child, or the
     child's potential melt-down causes the parent to abandon
     the agenda altogether. Neither decision is optimal because
     both are based on fear. The outcome is a more difficult,
     controlling child, or a child who feels no control of his own
     life's decisions. Both lack Grace.

Step 5: Execution

1.   Optimal Response: The child chooses a number of toys to
     part with and participates in taking the toys to a shelter or
     other depository where, potentially, he can see the
     outcome of his decision.
2.   Sub-Optimal Response: As they go through the toys, the
     child still cannot choose any toys that he is willing to do
     without and continues to cling to his belongings.

What Should Happen: Handled correctly, this child should enjoy a process
that initially created fear. There are different ways than those suggested
above to achieve the same outcome; however the outcome should always
be light and effortless.

Your **most** powerful outcome is achieved when you are able to find and
address the deepest level of fear. For example, it may look like the child's
fear is about loss, or not having enough, when it may really be about loss of
control and being at the whim of adults. Sometimes discovering the
deepest fear can feel like an Easter Egg hunt. You will know when you
have found and addressed the correct fear because the child relaxes. He
approaches the interaction with enthusiasm, or minimally, peace rather
than fear and hostility. You are never at Grace until you get to the deepest

levels of fear.

What Can Go Wrong: Because this is a five-step, repeating process there are multiple opportunities for error. For example, if the mother assumes that she has reached agreement, but in fact, she has worked her will with the child, the process will fall apart in execution. The child will fight again when dealing with the reality of giving away the toys.

The child's resistance is symptomatic of a problem somewhere in the previous steps. Perhaps the parent did not really understand or was not interested in what the child was feeling or saying. Such an outcome can throw the situation back into a new critical moment containing the same opportunities to arrive at Grace. Of course, the other option is to continue with the cycle of unhappy and intense emotional response.

How to Fix It: When you run into a critical moment, go back to the gifts of Grace. As the adult, she is both doing and teaching in this example. She should model the behaviors of flexibility, curiosity, and trust in her attempts to find solutions that meet everyone's need. Being arbitrary may get her a quick result, but it may make things harder in the long run. In your own situations, if you think the process is moving along and suddenly things become stuck in negative emotions, you need to back-track through the process, review and be sure that you have acted optimally at each step.

The Challenge: There are always multiple paths to any solution containing varying degrees of Grace. Patience is going to be the biggest challenge when you are dealing with a less evolved personality, in this case a child. The mother must also remember that she, too, has hidden fears. As the adult, do she possibly fear losing control of the child as much or more than the child fears losing control of his destiny? If so, she will need to work the process on herself, find her fear, isolate it and resolve to exercise curiosity, flexibility, and trust.

The Skill Set: The most important skill set in this particular situation is the ability to ask questions to help the child identify what he is really afraid of. The mother should assume that whatever he tells her is not necessarily the real fear and her job is going to be to find her way through his responses to find out what is really going on. (This inability to know and express the real nature of the fear is not isolated to children).

The Larger Implications

Not only is this child at a critical moment in terms of determining whether or not to cooperate with the culling of his toys. At a macro level he is processing his life's journey. He is learning to respond in real time to challenges to his sense of trust, clarity and confidence. He is forming patterns for his life.

Each and every critical moment grants us opportunities to reform our understanding and to proceed with curiosity, flexibility and detachment. Doing so gets harder as we get older which is one of the reasons the journey to Grace (reality) can be so demanding.

What you do with your own critical moments is your choice. Start with the assumption that you have the power to reverse any lessons that cause you the most pain, the most confusion and the most isolation from others. If you do so, you will be ahead of those who travel blindly through the gifts we are offered each and every day.

This is work. It is not easy, nor is it quick. You are looking for toe holds as you climb a cliff toward the top of a mountain and each toe hold only grants you permission to look for the next.

The structure of this book is intended to offer you examples and practice on issues of increasing complexity and difficulty. In the index you will find an in depth discussion of each of the five-steps of the cycle including challenges and objectives for each step. In the following chapters the work toward Grace is offered in a simple repetitive format so you can get accustomed to a process that you may wish to adopt as your own.

Things to keep in mind:

1.   **There are no "correct" responses to critical moments, nor are there formulas. Responses are creations based on the variables**

given in the moment. To find Grace is a process.

2. Interaction with others means you are managing two processes at once: yours and that of the other participants'.

3. Your levels of understanding, effectiveness and skill will evolve over time. What seems like vast improvement today may look like kindergarten from your future state of Grace.

Chapter V

Super-Positioning and the Great Short Cut

Becoming Hot Lava

We are about to increase the stakes yet again. Keep reminding yourself that Grace is an evolving cognitive understanding of yourself and the workings of the Universe. With each gain in understanding, you evolve your own levels of Confidence in yourself, Trust in the divine order of things, and Clarity about how all the pieces of each situation fit into the larger whole.

Being in Grace changes the experience of the repeating cycle and leaves you momentarily in what we will call *Super-Positioning*. Super-Positioning is a concept borrowed from Quantum Physics, in which a particle under examination is in a state of potential to be all places at once. For our purposes, you are in a position (or state of potential) from which you can see in any direction and you know how all the variables will be affected by any move you might make. Think of this state as a state of "all knowing". Super-Positioning is a state of heightened awareness achieved by the ultimate degrees of Confidence, Clarity and Trust. It is the gift of Grace.

The visioning and assessment steps can be instantaneous, calling for little or no processing. You immediately lift yourself above the knee-jerk reactions that occur when you feel insecure, and instead, you *know* what to do and you know that it is right. There is no indecisiveness, only Clarity, Confidence and Trust.

The result of such a state is to create a reality for you and your efforts that we will call *Hot Lava*. You are in a state of effortless flow and nothing can resist your force. You have an almost uncanny sense of all the energies around you and how to move in a way which enhances your opportunities to do and say the right things. You become the unstoppable force but you move with a beauty and awesome power to overcome obstacles.

Perhaps you have felt Super-Positioning with others when the team comes together and everyone is in sync and every moment resonates with Grace.

In athletics, they might call the state of Super-Positioning "being in the Zone" or Peak Performance. Hot Lava is the outcome. No one can stop you.

Naturally this state is rare and requires additional skill to achieve, particularly as you move through the five-step process and begin to engage with others.

What can you do to increase your odds of reaching Super-Positioning through Grace? You should always remember that your processing of the Critical Moment may be done internally. Ideally, when you know by your own negative emotions that you have entered a Critical Moment, you *won't* allow yourself to interact with others until you enter the stage of Engagement. Think things through carefully before being seduced into a response. This private space will increase your odds of overcoming your own weaknesses before adding the dimension of meeting the needs of others to the mix.

Once you enter the engagement step where actual decisions are made, you may find the need to test the perfection of what you feel. The process now becomes interactive and the potential for friction begins. During this step you interact with the variables of others' lives as well as your own.

Each moment is a moment of opportunity to take the situation to a state of Grace. The process is more complicated once the dance includes others, but is still doable. In order to arrive at Super-Positioning while engaged with others, you must attain a higher level of awareness and be inside of their needs as well as your own. (Throughout the rest of this text we will refer to understandings and advice that may help you achieve the state of Super-Positioning as *Advanced Intelligence*.)

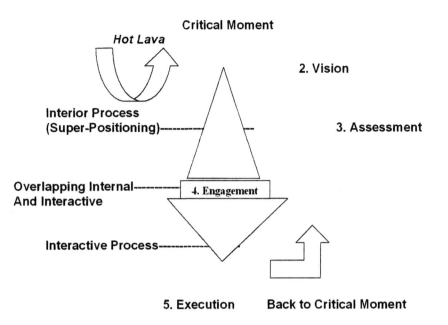

Critical Moment

Hot Lava

2. Vision

Interior Process
(Super-Positioning)--------- 3. Assessment

Overlapping Internal---------   4. Engagement
And Interactive

Interactive Process-----------

5. Execution   Back to Critical Moment

The rest of this chapter will deal with how to fix issues with Confidence, Clarity and Trust. You will be using the five-steps and Advanced Intelligence so that you may move to a state of Super-Positioning, and therefore, Grace more spontaneously and effortlessly.

Review the Steps with Super-Positioning In Mind

Step 1: Critical Moment
Begin the process by recognizing that you are entering a critical moment and identify both the feeling and the possible personal pattern in the fears you may be experiencing in the moment. Hopefully, you can immediately move into a state of Grace simply by finding your confidence, your trust, and your clarity in that moment. If not, deliberately continue on into Vision.

Step 2: Vision
Begin the visioning process by working from the most idealistic sense of what should happen. That does not necessarily mean envisioning getting your way or the demise of others, it means envisioning the best possible scenario. Worst case scenarios are totally inappropriate. Grace is Grace, after all.

Step 3: Assessment
In light of possible patterns identified in Step 1, you must remain curious, open, and gather as much data as possible before making any decisions. Identify your knee-jerk response and the risk of pursuing that option since it is most often the option based on fear. Try to identify what you *should* do and if there is something holding you back from automatically pursuing that option. Observe how the perceived risks stack up. Are they real? How do they measure up against the risk of doing the wrong thing? How do they differ in terms of long-term risk and short-term risk?

Step 4: Engagement
This step is where the process often becomes more interactive. When you begin engagement, you interact with those affected by the issue. You may have to repeat the visioning and assessment process with them, but you will still maintain a private interior dialogue around your vision, assessment and engagement (deciding).

This is an active, sometimes multi-level step if others are involved. The more openly curious and flexible you remain, and the more detached you are from bias, the more effective your style and results will be. The engagement step is both internal and sometimes interactive. You are making decisions in your head as well as entering into agreements with others. Their fear will play a part and obviously increase the complexity of managing the moment. When you have found your way to Trust, Confidence and Clarity, you will automatically flow through any resistance.

Step 5: Execution
This is the action step. You must make the moves you have decided upon and you must make them successfully. Problems will most certainly come

up if you have not been in a completely confident, clear, and trusting mode when you created your vision, analyzed your options and made your decisions. Work the process of the five steps repeatedly on any problems surfacing in the execution phase. You should attempt, at every iteration, to reach for Super-Positioning. In other words return to Vision and attempt to move any issues into Super-Positioning as quickly as possible. You will repeat the process of creating a vision, assessing the risks and deciding your actions, for each uncomfortable moment. The quicker you can react to the uncomfortable moments, the more effective your execution will be. This is the play within the play and each result takes you back to the top.

You will often dialogue with others during this step. Remain true to yourself and at the same time, open to others. You will make the decisions based on your assessment of the risks and data available to you. You can stay in control of whether a situation is moving toward Grace by attempting to keep your own thoughts in a Super-Positioning state. You cannot control the responses of others, but by remaining in control of yourself, you up the odds of a significantly improved outcome!

In every journey, large or small, you will go through the five-steps of the cycle, consciously or unconsciously. When moving from one step to the next, you will affect the direction by consciously choosing fear or Grace. By choosing fear, you choose the negative potential inherent in the moment and the results will be negative. By choosing to act with Confidence, Clarity and Trust you will move through each step on a path to Grace.

Creating Discipline around Confidence, Clarity and Trust

Think of your life process like the self-correct program on your word processor. For those of us who are dyslexic and therefore continually misspelling the same words, identifying the mistake as it occurs and adding it to the quick correct list causes the computer to recognize the problem the next time and automatically make the correction. Over time, you can go faster and faster as the computer is anticipating and correcting more and more of the errors which used to slow you down.

Hopefully the information you gain each time you handle a critical moment with Grace is now part of the programming in your brain. The next time it may not even occur as a critical moment, or at the very least, you recognize the problem as internal. You approach it more thoughtfully and your odds go up of handling it with Grace. Your objective is to increase the speed at which you move into Super Position (integration of Clarity, Confidence and Trust), thereby reducing the pain and chaos in your life.

Remember:

- **Grace is a discipline, not an accident.**
- **Your biggest opportunities to create flowing, effortless outcomes are at the beginning of the cycle when the steps are done internally.**
- **Short cutting to Grace is done by deciding early in the dance not to respond with fear.**
- **Super-Positioning is when you find yourself in that state where Clarity, Confidence, and Trust occur simultaneously regardless of what is happening in your life. It is the gift of Grace which allows you to be all-knowing about what is occurring around you.**
- **Hot Lava is the description of the power which is yours to command when you have reached Super-Positioning through Grace.**

Chapter VI

Finding Clarity, Confidence, and Trust in a Crisis

Assume every critical moment or crisis is a breakdown in your personal Confidence, Clarity or Trust. In order to cope with Grace, your job is to identify and fix the breakdown. Some breakdowns are small and some indicate core deficits that have occurred during your evolution as a human being.

It is a part of being human to experience loss of confidence in ones' self, the circumstance, others, etc. How you move through a loss of confidence determines whether you are able to return to Grace. At each step of the cycle you need to revisit your status within each fundamental component. Only when they are all present are you operating at your highest potential (Super-Positioning).

In the following case study we will work the process of the five-steps. We will employ the three fundamental components of Grace within each of the steps to show just how they *might* affect a person's response. At the end of the case study, you will find some questions you can ask yourself to help find Clarity, Confidence and Trust in your own crisis.

Case Study:

A very talented woman in a high level position in corporate America was disliked by many of her peers. She was actually a kind, funny, and generous personality. For some reason unknown to her she seems to repeatedly, throughout her career make her peers angry.

She has a strong sense of fairness and is incensed when she finds out that several of her peers have had a meeting with her subordinates without checking in with her. The woman's lack of confidence in her interactive skills and in her ability to generate loyalty fuels her sense of rage.

Feeling disliked is too familiar and her perception of threat regarding this situation is very high. This kind of situation might cause her to lash out at her subordinates and attempt to make them respond in a specific way which would make her feel safe.

Her instinctive response is also to get her boss involved to protect her and confront her peers on their behavior. This case study starts at the moment she finds out about the meeting.

*****

How should she handle the situation? Instead of following her instincts, which could be highly dysfunctional, she has the potential to 'up her odds' of a desirable outcome if she slows down, follows the five-step process and heeds the issues of her own confidence, clarity, and trust at each step.

- She should carefully work through the five-steps of the cycle, starting with identifying what she is feeling about this moment and why.
- In each step, she must identify what it would look like if she were confident, clear, and trusting in herself and the unfolding process (as opposed to fearful and controlling).
- To help her identify her ideal of Confidence, Clarity and Trust she can focus on the optimizing response for each fundamental component. For example, each time the woman finds herself responding from fear she must remind herself to be:

- Curious to gain clarity.
- Flexible to promote confidence.
- Detached from bias that dictates a specific outcome or drives her to guess at what is motivating her peers. She really does not know and her guesses may be highly destructive products of her own insecurities rather than reality.
  - She must challenge herself to act from the ideal of Confidence, Clarity and Trust no matter how compulsive or fearful she is feeling.
  - She must check the result she is getting each step of the way. If the process does not feel like an effortless flow, she should

revisit where she is in the cycle and identify where and how she is operating from fear.

An Application of the Process with a Focus on Grace

I.   Critical Moment

If she were coming from a place of Confidence, Clarity and Trust, what would she be feeling now?
- Puzzled that they didn't just tell her what they were thinking. A sense that she must not have enough information because their behavior makes no sense.
- A certainty that they must be feeling very insecure or they would have behaved differently.
- A concern that her people do not get caught in the middle.
- A strong belief that the Universe is bringing her this so she can solve a problem early before it becomes more destructive.

II.   Vision

If she is confident, clear and trusting of the Universe, what is the most ideal vision totally within *her* control and not dependent on the reactions of others? This might be an example:

- She will wish to be able to identify which aspects of her behavior/attitude/demeanor make her peers use subterfuge to get around her. She will adopt a more powerful style that they do not wish to attack.
- She and her peers will always talk openly about the problems between them and make resolutions to fix them.
- She will find effective ways to listen to and to accommodate the needs of the people with whom she works and they will know it and act more openly as a result.
- Long-term: She will decide to only work among people she respects and who respect her. She will take the appropriate risks to make that a reality.

III.   Assessment

If she is feeling confident (not threatened), clear and trusting, what will she do to gather information before taking any definitive steps?

- She will ask her peers if there is something she has been neglecting that caused them to go around her. She will ask how she and her team can better serve their needs.
- From their suggestions, she will identify her own limitations in resources or skills and ask for their help in coping with those limitations.
- She will ask herself whether she has spent enough energy building her peer relationships and what she needs to do to improve those relationships.
- She will ask her employees how she can support them in interacting with her peers.

Next, she enters the interactive phase (engagement) with her peers where she must continually make decisions *in the moment* about how the situation is going to play out. Being aware of the fears of her peers, as well as her own fears, adds enormous complexity to the situation. It becomes even more difficult to maintain Grace because she does not always have time to process how she wants to react to their responses.

Ideally, if unsure or undecided, she will take a time out. She will give herself the gift of time to think and, therefore, to avoid being rushed into bad behavior.

IV.   Engagement

If she has a strong sense of personal confidence, if she trusts that the unfolding process will only strengthen her and her long-term position, and if she is clear about her peers' motivations, she might handle this step as follows:

- She will approach the entire situation openly and without bias toward a particular outcome. She will also identify and let go of her biases about her peers. (Very Difficult! That's why it is called Grace.)

- To give her peers a greater feeling of responsiveness from her team, she will ask them to help her decide next steps for her team. They will discuss solutions to the problems and follow a process of vision and assessment together. Note that the next step indicates what she can do if she does not like their suggestions.
- She will respond from Clarity and Confidence to their requests. Where she feels it isn't possible or positive to meet their specific requests, she will ask for alternatives which still meet their needs. She will be clear about why she is feeling unable to do exactly what they asked. In other words, she will not cave in just to be liked. Instead she will work with them to find solutions that work for her too.

V.   Execution

If she starts with a strong sense of personal Confidence, Trust and Clarity, how will she handle the problems which are certain to surface during the execution of whatever plan the group creates?
- She will stay very attentive to what is happening, how she is feeling, how her peers are feeling, how her subordinates are feeling, and ultimately, whether the plan is producing satisfactory results.
- If an emotional response is triggered at any point in the process, she will immediately review the internal process of envisioning an ideal and assessing her options before re-engaging with others to fix whatever is going wrong.

Remember, the woman's instinctive response was to assume that her peers' choice to go around her was a bid to rob her of authority. From that perspective, her (undisciplined) vision would be subconsciously attracted toward worse case scenarios such as predicting that she would end up with a smaller organization as a result of their turf war. While this is not necessarily unrealistic (it had happened in the past), it is not a vision that will create the most Graceful response from her and may actually increase the odds of her worst fear taking place. Her knee-jerk responses are highly likely to be angry and controlling and would undoubtedly exacerbate the original, deviant behaviors of her peers.

We are not suggesting that the responses above are the absolute best or only responses. What is being suggested is that you can improve your odds for a better outcome if you work through a process with your eye on the three fundamental components of Grace.

You must find your way to your personal Confidence, your Clarity in tough moments and your Trust in the unfolding events because they are unique to your life's experience and your beliefs. However, here are some very simple techniques and thought processes which may help you. Keep in mind that these three concepts are intricately woven together so there will undoubtedly be overlap.

CLARITY

Curiosity

Symptoms	Possible individual Cause/Belief	Possible Response to Return to Grace
Confusion	• Moving too quickly to solutions (engagement) without knowing what you want or gathering enough info. • Being misled by devious people.	• Revisit Vision and Assessment steps. Are your decisions in line with what you say you want? Have you correctly analyzed the risks of a decision? Have you correctly analyzed risk of doing nothing? • Do not be naive. When you have information that says specific individuals are not trustworthy, gather more info whenever dealing with them. This is also true of people you are close to if they have given you reason to mistrust. You can trust the Universe, but you must also trust yourself and what you know. • Do nothing until confusion clears. Explore until you have enough info. Do not be rushed!

Indecisive	• Being afraid of failure. Watch for this as a pattern. • Perfectionism. • Lack of trust in your ability to deal with issues as they arise. • Lack of personal confidence.	• Identify whether your indecisiveness is related to not having enough information or a crisis in your own sense of self. • If it is a self esteem issue, work on your self-confidence while working the issue. Challenge yourself to take risks on the kinds of things that you know you have been successful on in the past.

• Haunted by choices.	• Fear of loss.	• Identify what you are *really* afraid of and weigh the consequences of not letting go. Go back to the Assessment step and identify the risk of holding on vs. moving on.
• Constant revisiting of decisions rather than getting on with it.	• Lack of trust in the information you have.	
• Pattern of clarity and then of becoming confused when in the midst of action.	• Inability to be objective or maintain emotional detachment.	
	• Clinging to the past.	• Imagine that you are making the decision for someone else. What would you advise them?
	• Incomplete development in setting boundaries to protect own interests.	
		• If you are bad at setting boundaries, get tougher. Pretend that you are advising your child on how to handle this particular person and circumstance. What would you do differently for them than you would do for yourself?
		• Go back to the Vision step and get a much clearer vision of what you have to look forward to when completing this lesson. Make sure you make it ideal.

Assuming the other person's intentions.	You may be operating from insecurity, fear or lack of trust in the Universe.	Assume that the other person's issues are not about you. Be curious about what fear is driving the other person so you can create the best response. Assume they are pawns of the Universe to move you to another path.
Leaping to worst case outcome.	• Practice in having done so. • Need to break negativity as a pattern.	• Assume that you can handle whatever comes your way. • Identify what you would do if the worse case happens and then create a plan that diminishes your need to do so.

This table is not intended to answer all of your questions when addressing issues of clarity. It is meant to offer suggestions and starting places for your journey. The next table addresses the issues of confidence in a similar fashion. Keep in mind, once again, that there will be many overlapping concepts.

CONFIDENCE

Flexibility

Symptom	Cause/Belief	Possible Response
Avoiding confrontation.	• Too easily taken off-track when attempting to confront. • Too often end up defending yourself when you confront others. • Afraid that you might be wrong.	• Learn how to stick to the point when confronting. • Take the conversation right back to the topic at hand. • Assume that you may be wrong but describe your issues in terms of how he or she is making you feel. A person cannot argue with your feelings and they will be forced to deal with how you are interpreting their behavior.
• Need to be liked. • Neediness.	• Fear that if people do not like you or like what you do, then you will not be successful. • You do not feel you are enough if others do not like you. • Stuck in getting approval from those who do not deserve your good will. • Afraid for your security.	• Let go of (be flexible around) whatever keeps you in the approval dance with these people. • If they control your career, think about a new career. • If they control where or how you live, give yourself permission to live somewhere else. • Don't get stuck. • Get flexible (less stuck and more creative) around whatever you believe you cannot change around this situation.

• Not worthy of positive treatment from others. • Expectation of negative treatment.	• Stuck in old belief about you. • Depending on others. • Old tapes in your head about your self worth.	• Get professional help around self esteem. • Be flexible regarding what you believe forces you to stay and take bad treatment from others (e.g. I won't have a place to live, enough money, someone to care for my child, etc.). • Stop being stuck in the details; get more creative about how to meet your needs.
Feeling judged by others.	Assuming that others judge you as harshly as you judge others.	• Be more flexible with your acceptance of self and others. • Assume you are not always right. • Assume there are multiple means to an end.
Highly critical of others.	Usually insecurity causes this.	See above.

TRUST

Non-biased detachment

Symptoms	Cause/belief	Response
Controlling responses to critical moments.	If I do not take control, my position will be undermined.	Believe that all that occurs is ultimately being worked out to help you or benefit you.
Fear about the future.	• No sense of your own ability to cope or respond to things that may go wrong. • No sense of larger force or power that is in perfect order.	• Observe the past for how things right themselves over time to gain confidence in the future. • Look for patterns in your own historical ability to confront tough times and make sense of them. • Trust in your own talents and abilities to handle change and obstacles. • Build your own plans for things you fear and then put your fear aside.
Fear of missing something or making a mistake.	• Fear of failure. • Overstated fear of cost of mistakes or failures. • History of being blamed for mistakes.	• Watch for how the mistakes or failures evolve into paths you might have missed. • Build a list of such things. • Choose to see evidence of those mistakes that create *needed* change in direction.

Assumption that things will go badly.	• Belief in a hostile Universe. • Low self esteem and/or lack of confidence in ability to manage difficulty.	Decide to be optimistic. Perhaps you will be wrong, but your mood and therefore capacity to handle things will be better with that belief. It is your choice.
Constant sense of dread.	Bad things really do happen; your turn will come.	Assume that there is always a greater and larger purpose. Look for it!
Overreaction to the moves and choices of others or anything that takes away your control.	• Possible reaction to something in the past where control was taken away and consequences to psyche were severe. • Learned behavior.	• Get clarity about actual seriousness of the consequences of particular situation vs. your knee-jerk reaction. • Create your plan for if the worst should happen and be ready vs. afraid. • Allow for the Universe intervening on your behalf and see if you can identify how that might be.

Things to Remember:

1.   Take a good look at your life. If you are living in conflict and struggle, assume that your beliefs and your instincts are serving you poorly.

2.   Make a decision to act as though you are learning anew about how the world works. Apply trust, clarity and confidence and see whether you get a different result.

3.   If what you are doing is not working, do not do more of it.

PRACTICE APPLICATIONS IN BEHAVING WITH GRACE

Forgiving means to pardon the unpardonable.
Faith means believing the unbelievable.
Hoping means to hope when things are hopeless.

~~~G.K. Chesterton

Why Practice?

Responding with Grace takes practice. What if you found out today that the tooth ache you have been ignoring was really a rare form of cancer in a particularly hard to reach part of your head? Are you ready? Would you respond with Clarity, Confidence and Trust? Would you respond with those three qualities if you found out that this particular form of Cancer was probably going to run its course no matter what intervention you were willing to subject yourself to? The purpose of practice is:

1.   **To gain proficiency with the skills and understandings of Grace.** Think about the way you react now to obstacles, controlling behavior of others, or to being out of control. Do you react with a smooth and effortless flow to those things that distress you most? If not, how do you expect to react to those things upon which the very quality of your life may depend?

2.   **To establish a basis (belief system) to help you with the most complicated of life's challenges.** As you work with the examples in this book you may find that your beliefs about how the world works are replaced with new, more helpful beliefs which allow you to find a better, more optimal response to issues that challenge your self-confidence and skills.

3.   **To develop a level of fitness in your ability to handle crisis appropriately.** Since your confidence in *you* will greatly determine the difference between fear-based controlling responses and effortless, fluid reactions to difficult situations, practice may help you evolve your personal sense of power in situations that are difficult.

Clarify your Goals for this Work

In each of the following examples, you will be given an objective. Your job is to identify what you personally want to learn or take away from this work. In other words, who do you want to be, how do you want to grow, how would you like to be affected as a result of focusing on the amount of Grace that you exhibit in difficult situations?

69

You may want to become calmer, more tranquil. For others, the objective may be to be more clear, more directed, less easily influenced by others. It will be different for each person, and as a result, the work will be specifically yours to design.

For each exercise you will be given a direction, an approach, a sense of what should happen if you do things correctly (with Grace). You will also be given a warning about what can go wrong along with tips on how to fix it.

The entire set of applications is divided into three major segments. These segments are directly related to the three fundamentals of Grace, with each of the three segments focusing on one of the fundamentals.

Levels of Grace

In each of the following applications, you will be guided through a sequence of steps designed to help you think about an issue. The issue is yours; the steps are only a guide. The guide asks you to examine the issue using the five-steps of the cycle. It is always a good starting place. Your task will be to determine whether the reality of your issue is related to being out of sequence or out of Trust, Confidence and Clarity.

You will be warned about common errors in judgment or action. You must decide if the warnings fit with your situation. You will want to look hard for your blind spots in order to correct for issues that have repeatedly caused you discomfort or grief without you realizing your own culpability.

You will work on issues you choose. The applications are designed to reveal higher and higher levels of response as you work through them. In each section you will find a comment on Advanced Intelligence. This represents the understandings and actions of a person who has spent a lot of time studying and working with Grace.

Since real Grace is achieved through mastery, you may find that you improve your ability to handle critical moments gradually, one level at a time. For that reason, the applications section of this text is organized into two levels (*Level I and Level II*).

Level II applications are harder. You may not think so at first, but they *are* harder. You will find your ability to remain unbiased, clear headed and confident more severely challenged in the Level II exercises. Remember, symptoms of stress, disease, tension, etc. that you may experience are all clues that you are struggling in the cycle. Be kind to yourself and return to the cycle of steps to identify where your fear led you astray.

Built into the structure of the applications is a gradual increase of sophistication in understanding Grace. As you work through the exercises in sequence, you will be challenged to understand Clarity, Confidence, and Trust in more depth.

This is intentional. Some of the thinking introduced along the way may challenge your current assumptions about how life works. Practice the concepts even if you are not convinced they are true. Observe the difference in how your life functions. If you find yourself repelled by some of the assumptions you are asked to embrace, remember that Grace is an absence of rigidity. Try things you would not necessarily try as a way of stretching yourself and your understanding.

You always have the option of trashing anything that does not fit. Just wait to trash it until *after* you have tried it.

Remember:

1.   **If you really knew everything there is to know about how life works, life would be easy. If your life is not easy, try new things.**

2.   **These applications are about *your* life. Think of the rest of this text as a guide to understanding *your* life. Try not to hurry through them.**

3.   **If you do not journal, try it. It is always interesting to go back and analyze your growth.**

Applications for Specific Problems

The following issues can be addressed by any one of the applications listed behind it. You will find it helpful to simply choose one of the exercises and go through the process. As you re-address the same issue over time, try different exercises to discover different aspects of the issue. All of our issues are symptomatic of our misaligned perspectives and beliefs. As you identify and work through them, you will find that resolving the issues is like peeling an onion. You will work it through at one level, only to find yourself struggling with the same issue at another level.

- Professional anxiety: Applications # 3-20
- Relationship Angst: Applications # 1, 3, 4,-20
- Stubbornness: Applications # 2, 3, 4, 9, 10, 12, 14, 16, 17, 18, 19, 20
- Sadness/despair: Applications # 4, 9, 10, 12, 13, 14, 20
- Insecurity: Applications # 1-14, 16, 17, 20
- Controlling Behavior: Applications # 1, 2, 3, 6, 7, 9, 12, 13, 14,15,16,17,18, 20
- Aggressive behavior, Bullying: Applications # 1, 3, 4, 5, 7, 9, 11, 14, 15, 16,18,20
- Confusion/false starts: Applications #3, 5, 9, 12, 13, 14, 15, 18, 19, 20
- Disrespect: Applications # 1, 4, 5, 6, 7, 9, 14, 15, 16, 17, 18, 20
- Health Crisis: Applications # 3, 6, 7, 9, 10, 14, 20
- Financial Crisis: Applications # 3-11, 13, 14, 18, *20
- Misunderstanding the signals: Applications # 3, 4, 9, 10, 12, 14, 16, 17, 19
- Diminishing others to gain your objectives: # 8, 9, 10, 11, 15, 18, 19

* Exercise #20 is particularly important for Financial Crisis

Confidence

Application #1

Saying "NO" to Difficult People

Establishing appropriate boundaries is difficult for most of us with certain individuals. For some of us this is a pattern. Wherever it exists in your life it is worth exploring the root cause. You will find out things about who you are that will be helpful on your journey to more consistently flowing behavior.

Objective:

- To understand and more effectively manage your blind spots so others cannot take advantage of you.
- To create more give and take in your life with specific individuals who are problematic for you.
- To create a sense of your own equality with others.
- Flexibility.
- Clarity without intimidation.
- Trust in the order of things without being passive.

Prepare:

Define Your Initiative:

Identify a person who intimidates you or with whom you have a difficult time saying "No". Identify a specific situation in which you want to say "No" but feel you cannot or will not for whatever reason.

Write a brief description of what you will work on in your journal!

The Challenge:

The biggest challenge in saying "No" is dealing with the fact that other people won't like it when they do not get their way. They especially will not like it if they have become accustomed to you being compliant. Expect them to fight back, resist your attempt to set boundaries and possibly exhibit a form of temper tantrum. Do not allow these behaviors to muddle your Clarity. This practice is not for the faint of heart!

(Avoid passive-aggressive attempts to work your will. That is not Grace!)

The Skill Set:

An important skill in this situation is the ability to offer options *excluding* the one you are saying "No" to. Get clear about what the other person really needs as opposed to what they say they want. Offer them a peace offering that feels good to you.

For example, if your child wants the car for an evening with friends and you are concerned that he or she is not ready for the responsibility; trust yourself (unless your issue is that you are a control freak-that's a different test). You might say, "I am saying "No" because I do not feel that you've arrived at the judgment and skill level I think you need for this kind of outing. Instead we can take your friends to the Mall this weekend and we will see how it goes.

Don't argue. Offer a suggestion as a means to an end and give yourself plenty of opportunity to see if they use their responsibilities with wisdom. Don't give in until you believe they are ready. Do not fear the response. You are not in a popularity contest.

Approach:

Examine the five-step process for information:

Critical Moment: Be specific about the nature of your feelings regarding interactions with this person when you want to say "No". In other words, what is the nature of this critical moment? Are you angry? Are you afraid? Do you become confused by the way the other person maneuvers you into corners?

Vision: Identify a vision for how you would like the interaction to go. Make sure that it is a vision of you saying "No" *effectively*. Do not seek easy outs. Having the problem simply go away is not a vision that will bring your skill level up sufficiently to handle future problems.

Assessment: Assess the risks carefully to identify what you are really afraid of. Identify what you think will happen if you do not say "No" and what will happen if you do. Whatever you identify as the result of saying "No" is the risk you are avoiding. What does it cost you to continue to avoid taking that risk? Is it really such an awful outcome when compared to what you are feeling?

Execution: Make a resolution to take the risk, skillfully (see *Skill Set* above), no matter what your fear.

- Imagine that you say "No" and then evaluate your feelings. Are you afraid? Are you dreading their response? Are you already wondering if it was worth it?

Outcomes:

What Should Happen:

Handled correctly, this person should accept that you are saying "No" and should not continue to pressure you to do something you do not want to do. If you are able to say "NO" with Confidence, Clarity, and Trust, the other person should understand and honor your reasons for saying "No".

What Can Go Wrong:

- You may attempt to say "No" before dealing with your underlying fear and it will come off as not confident or as if you don't really mean what you are saying. The other person will sense your weakness and find a way to manipulate you.
- If you lack a sense of your own worth or of your right to say "No", a bully will back you into a corner.
- If the person has positional power over you, you may not have done enough homework in your analysis phase and now find that the risk of

losing your job, marriage or place in the world causes you to weaken when you need to be strong. You must resolve these deep fears before you tackle your nemesis or you will probably end up "eating crow."

- You may say "No" and then feel haunted with guilt afterwards.

How to Fix It:

If you get a negative result from saying "No" when saying "No" is justified, then return to the five-steps.

Confirm that your vision of the outcome was fully formed. Did your vision stop with saying "No" or did you create a vision of the entire outcome?

Were you confident in your right to say "No"? Did you fully assess the risks?

When you were in the process of saying "No" (engagement and execution) were you clear, definitive and unequivocal? Remember that arguing over your reasons is a symptom of weakness. Do not enter into endless dialogue about why you are taking care of yourself. It creates the sense that you are uncertain of your right to say what you feel. There is a saying you may want to keep in mind: "Never explain. Your friends don't need it and your enemies won't believe you!"

One of the most critical errors in this particular exercise is when you do not fully analyze the risks and deal with them before you take action. For example, if you are afraid that saying "No" will cost you your marriage are you prepared for *that* when you say "No"? If you are not prepared to handle some level of risk, the other person will sense it and exploit your fear.

Try practicing on smaller things if the big ones are too risky. The inability to protect your boundaries is a life-long issue and deserves gradual development.

Advanced Intelligence:

Your **most** powerful outcome will surface when you are able to find and address your deepest level of fear. For example, you may accommodate this person due to a deep fear of being alone. It is probable that you have lived with and made decisions based on this fear for a long time.

Initially, it may feel as though you are doing something very wrong, disrespectful or damaging to yourself to say "No". Ultimately you will realize that the best outcome-not only for you but also for the others involved-is when you are true to yourself.

You will begin to observe that when you are clear and not afraid to say "No" the other person's life is also better as a result. This occurs when you do what is right so beautifully that the other person does not feel it as a fight for control or dominance.

Boundary issues are usually about fear. The answers are always within the three fundamentals of Grace. Try to identify your fear. Next, identify why you would not face that fear rather than accept that another person controls you so completely. Imagine what your life would be like if you no longer had that fear and attempt to act as if you were already there. Do it on small things so that you will be prepared to attempt it on the big things.

FREEDOM is a state of mind. A person of Grace is always free.

Below, I've included some possible tests of your Clarity, Confidence and Trust with potential solutions:

Issue	Possible Underlying Cause	Possible solutions
You cannot get past your fear of saying "No" to this person. You clutch at the thought.	You are afraid for your existence as a result of saying "No". This might include job security, family security, or fear that the other person will leave if they do not get their way. Have you looked at the chain of events you are afraid of unleashing by denying this person? Take the fear all the way to the subconscious level to find your weak spot.	Examine the real risk associated with the fear. Is it really as bad as you think it is? Could you be exaggerating this in your mind? If it really is that bad, are you aware that the other person is holding you hostage? What is the long-term risk if you continue to allow this? Compare risks and decide. Since the price you pay is diminished vitality, is it worth it?
The other person threatens you.	They believe that you will cave to their threats. If this were not the case, the threat would not come up. They sense this weakness in you and exploit it.	Do your homework. Imagine what the other person will do before you start the dialogue. Work through your fear before beginning and, if the person does what you fear, recognize out loud that the person *can* follow this path, but to do so may not achieve his or her objectives.
You say "No" and he or she ignores you and proceeds as if you have said "Yes".	You are not convinced of your right to say "No". The other person uses your low sense of Self to manipulate you.	Become curious about the mixed message you are sending. How is it that you are saying "No" and the other person hears "Yes"? Look at your other behaviors and see how you are allowing this condition.

Application #2

Level II

Do Something You are Afraid Of

There is a saying: "Do something you are afraid of every day."

Objective:
- To become more fluid doing things which cause you fear.
- To recognize them as challenges to your maturity and Grace instead of hindrances to your comfort level.
- To learn how to experience less fear of intense situations, and therefore, more ease in coping and going through them.
- To gain confidence in your own ability to manage tough circumstances. (This exercise may be particularly hard on you at the beginning, but it will definitely get easier if you practice. You will build and test "muscles" you do not even know you have.)
- To learn to keep what you fear in perspective within the larger scheme of things.
- To manage the larger pattern while you manage the event.

Prepare:

Define Your Initiative:

Choose to work on something that makes you uncomfortable, or even fearful. If you are choosing something physical, be sure to identify in the analysis step whether you are actually physically *capable* of what you are attempting. Do **NOT** put yourself in real danger to prove something to yourself. Always manage the risk of whatever you are tackling by being smart about it (Step 3, Analysis of the five-step cycle).

It might be better to choose to work through one of your negative patterns. For example, do you hate sharing your feelings? Do you hate losing control in personal situations? Are you nervous about giving others "too much" information? Do you dislike trusting others? There is usually more to

81

choose from than you might imagine. (Many of your fears control your behaviors while you remain unaware of their influence on your choices. It is a bit like a program running in the background on your computer.)

If you choose your practice initiative carefully, you will find this *Level II* Application more difficult than *Level I*. The fear you choose to work on for this application should be a fear you have lived with for a long time. Remember that you are attempting to find Clarity, Confidence, and Trust.

Write a brief description of what you will work on in your journal!

The Challenge: The real challenge is to identify a way to tackle this initiative differently than you have before. You will automatically gravitate to your old behaviors, which have not worked for you. You must assume that you are afraid for a reason and that you need to find your way through the fear so you are not left with even more reason to fear this circumstance. What do you fear most in this situation and what about your approach might cause that to happen?

The Skill Set: The most important thing you can learn to do is to relax under pressure. Utilizing breathing and mental relaxation techniques will assist you in getting a good result. Carrying tension into the execution phase will only cause you to react inappropriately if anything goes wrong. The ability to assess and respond quickly if you find things headed the wrong direction is critical. You will need to think things through in the beginning and stay clear and present during engagement and execution.

Approach:

Examine the five-step process:

Critical Moment: Identify the nature of your fear. What are you *really* afraid of? Is your fear realistic? If so, acknowledge that and resolve to work through it anyway.

Vision: Identify a vision for the outcome you want. Be sure to make it positive and doable. (Choose to break the initiative down into bite size pieces. Choose and analyze *a small piece* to start your work. Remember, you get to work on something you are afraid of every day. You do not have to do it all at once!)

Assessment: Identify the actual risks of the initiative and identify ways to diminish the risk while still acting within the three qualities of Grace. Be careful about approaching the issue in the old way. You are likely to get the old result.

Engagement: After you have carefully identified and accounted for the risks, make a decision of what you will do, how you will do it, and how you will know if it is working for you.

Execution: As you do whatever it is that you are afraid of, continue to examine your feelings and observe what surfaces in your emotional reactions.

Outcomes:

What Should Happen?

If you have been careful to break things down into manageable, bite size pieces, you should find that the issue that scared you before still makes you nervous but is now manageable. If you complete what you set out to do, you will feel lighter, satisfied and liberated. You should end up being a little more trusting of yourself and your ability to manage difficult circumstances as a result of your decisions and actions.

What Can Go Wrong:

- You could slip back into an old pattern as you attempt to execute.
- You could get the thing you fear.
- Your fear level could escalate and cause you to freeze at the wrong moment.
- You may not understand the true nature of why you are afraid. This would cause you to solve the wrong problem.

- If you take on more than you've prepared for you may start powerfully but then run into trouble by getting ahead of yourself.
- In managing your own fear you may become too aggressive and cause others in your process to over-react or to react negatively.
- You execute without remembering that it is an ongoing process and you must adjust moment to moment.

How to Fix It:

- Remain curious throughout the process. If it stops feeling as though it is working appropriately at any point, stop. Start asking questions. Why are others reacting as they are? Why are you doing what you are doing? Break it down until you understand what is going wrong. Don't wait until you get a bad result. That will only affirm your fear.
- If you have become rigid or controlling, stop. Ask yourself why. If others are involved, place yourself in their shoes and ask if you are going too far without giving them enough information about why you are doing what you are doing.
- Break the initiative into a smaller bite. Do not be in a hurry. Act as though you have your whole life to work through this problem. You do.
- Ask the question: How should this look and feel if I really get it right? Get a clear picture and then ask what you might do differently to achieve that end.
- Look at the problem from a macro point of view. If the Universe is presenting this particular problem as a gift to help you move your life to another level, what are the issues of cause and effect in operation?

Advanced Intelligence:

An interesting thing about working through fear is that whatever you choose to work on is often representative of a larger and more pervasive life fear. You may think of it as a metaphor for your life. For example, if you choose to work on sharing negative feelings with someone who has been making your life miserable, you may look at the entire pattern of your life and realize that you have a general tendency to hold back on your feelings as though they're not legitimate. Look for the larger pattern in the exercise you choose.

A light touch is always more effective than a heavy, over-controlling response to a situation that causes you fear. If you get in trouble, attempt to go against your instincts and try a lighter touch. Keep telling yourself to "lighten" when you want to "tighten". Push forward when you want to pull back. Think FORWARD, not back.

A few options for response are listed in the chart below:

Issue	Possible Underlying Cause	Possible Path Back to Grace
You have a sense of being "in over your head" and panic part way through.	You instinctively tightened up and then things went badly. This validates your fear and perpetuates the problem.	Slow everything down. Practice breathing deeply, clear your mind and identify what you are afraid of. Ask "why?" See if you can identify the underlying fear. Pick someone you respect and try to imagine how they would handle this moment. Try it.
All through the initiative you feel as if you are walking a tightrope and can hardly wait for it to be over.	Remember, you are doing this because you are afraid of it. That may happen the first few times you do it.	Be kind to yourself. Give yourself time to adjust. Attempt to identify the good things that are happening as they occur so that over time you are relaxed with this very thing that scares you. Acknowledge how brave you are.
You get a bad result and feel justified in your fear. You never actually work through the fear and you become bounded by it.	If you do not really understand the fear and what is causing it in the first place, you will remain clouded around the issue. This will block positive, flowing and effortless results.	Dive deeper into what you are afraid of. Look again for the larger life pattern and begin to put some effort into working with it as a pattern. Gain new insight and try again.

Application #3

When You Are in a Hurry and No One Else Gets It

Level 1

Timing represents a complicated, multifaceted area to explore for potential critical moments.

Objective:

- To understand and work effectively with issues of timing.
- Effortless flow.
- Calm and controlled and easy access to what you need.
- A sense of perfection in the timing of the Universe.

Prepare:

Define Your Initiative:

Pick an issue or circumstance around which you have a sense of urgency. You are in a hurry to make progress or complete and others are ambivalent or even resisting your sense of importance regarding the issue.

Write a brief description of what you will work on in your journal!

The Challenge: Timing issues are always indicative of other issues. The real challenge is getting to the root cause and knowing how to deal with it. Knowing yourself and whether or not your fear is driving your behavior is difficult but important. When you begin to deal with the fear instead of the urgency you *will* make progress.

The Skill Set: There are two critical skills you will need. First, you must be able to identify and solve the fears of others who are resisting you. Second, you must be able to identify and work with your own fears that are triggering your urgency in the first place. If the Universe is the entity

87

opposing you, step back and ask why you are not supposed to have this desired outcome right now.

Approach:

Examine the 5 step process:

Critical Moment: Identify whether this sense of urgency is a repeating pattern for you. Do you get this way often? Have you been wrong? Can you think of times when you pushed and it was not successful or times when you had to rework things because of your haste?

Identify what you are feeling regarding this situation. If you are feeling afraid, be specific as to the nature of the fear. Is it a fear of losing control? Is it a fear of being missing a window of opportunity? Have you put extraordinary pressure on this specific project to save the company, save the marriage, save your job? Is that pressure appropriate? If so, get more realistic regarding the relative value of this initiative. Do not make your reactions out of sync with reality.

Vision: Take the time to identify what it would feel like if everything was going perfectly. Be sure to include how others would react and interact with you around this situation if your sense of timing were perfect.

Assessment: Analyze the risk carefully. Much of the Grace within timing issues can be resolved with more appropriate risk assessment. What are you really afraid of regarding the timing of this initiative? Do you fear you will lose control of the initiative if you are not able to get the timing your way?

Start with the assumption that it is *perfect* that you are not getting your way easily on this timing issue. See if you can find out what the reason might be; it might be found somewhere within the five-steps of the cycle. For example, perhaps your vision is not yet clear, the decision is not concise or correct, others are not engaged or your assessment of risk is incorrect. Assume *you* are not yet ready, or something else is not ready for you to succeed.

Be curious. Ask others why they are reacting to you as they are. You may be ahead of them in the process. They may still be trying to assess the risk while you are pushing on to execution. Be sure that you clearly understand the problem.

Engagement: Try to get agreement regarding the timing. If agreement eludes you, see if there is another way to get to the outcome you seek. Be flexible, not rigid regarding what you want.

Execution: If you get agreement from others but they do not deliver, continue working back through the steps of the cycle until agreement means agreement. Watch your own behavior carefully for symptoms of pushing people to agreement before they are ready.

Outcomes:

What Should Happen: When you look at why the situation is not moving as fast as you would like it to, you should find something out of alignment. You may find that you have not done the work of getting others on board, or you have been too quick to assume their support or involvement. You may find that your plan is incomplete or has missed a key obstacle that others are trying to point out. Once you find what was out of order or incomplete in the cycle of steps, you should be able to put things in motion again. The pace may still feel too slow for you if "urgency" is one of your patterns.

What Can Go Wrong: You might find yourself trying to bully others to the outcome you seek. When you push for something against the flow, and before dealing with your fears, it will often backfire and cause you to wish you had slowed down and become curious. Suddenly, you will find that you have become the enemy and instead of singing your praises, others will vilify you. You may not get credit for saving the day, but instead be the recipient of negativity and condemnations of your character. What took heroic dedication from you may become the thing others hate you for. These are signs that you are out of Grace; out of flow.

How to Fix It: If you push through and get your way only to find yourself in the midst of a battle as a result of your urgency, become curious. Ask others what they felt when dealing with you. Identify the outcome of your behavior that is now affecting your result. Get clear with yourself on what your motives were. If they are self-serving in any way, own it, and then make a promise to yourself that you will be better in the future with your responsibility to remain more objective.

Advanced Intelligence:

Timing is rarely ours to decide. While we usually perceive timing to be within our control it hardly ever is. Timing is an issue of Trust.

If you are a rusher and everything has slowed down, try to imagine the benefits to you in slowing down your agenda. Look for clues in the environment that might show you why it has been to your advantage to have things slow down. Assume that the Universe is always in your favor and for some reason it deems you not yet ready for what you are asking. You will find substantial evidence to back that up if you stay authentic and are able to let go of your ego.

The following table will clarify some options:

Issue	Possible Underlying Cause	Path back to Grace
Others refuse to participate or complete something they agreed to.	You may have assumed others agreed when, in reality, you forced their hand or ignored their resistance.	Start a dialogue. Be careful not to fill in the blanks if they do not communicate initially. Wait for others to tell you what is going on. Be wary of trying to push others to agreement or to convince them.

Issue	Possible Underlying Cause	Path back to Grace
You have no sense of cooperation from others.	You have a sense of your own self-importance with little respect for the critical nature of how others are already spending *their* time.	Strive for objectivity or clarity about relative risks. Is it really as dire as you think? Is what you are working on really so much more important than what everyone else is working on?
Those who must give you permission to proceed are reluctant or refuse to do so.	• You are too enthusiastic without validating your position properly. • Others are protecting themselves in some way that you do not understand or respect.	• Spend more time doing your homework and validating your position. Be sure to weigh the risks more effectively for your audience. • Be very careful of attempting to work your will by inspiring through fear. It only works temporarily as a strategy.
You feel that others are stupid to not see how important this initiative really is.	You may have treated them as disrespectfully as you feel. They may be resisting you on principle.	Slow down. Find what it is that you respect about each person involved and begin to treat them with that in mind. Ask for what you need from them with a respect for their point of view. Be more open and curious regarding *they* want and need.
You have a pattern of feeling that things are urgent as well as a history of having others block your way.	You may be more intuitive than others, and as a result, are ahead of them in your thinking.	You may need to slow down, understand where others are, and then take them through a linear understanding of what you see.

Issue	Possible Underlying Cause	Path back to Grace
Same issue as above but a different cause.	You may hurry out of a fear of losing control of the initiative. You may be operating from fear rather than clarity or objectivity.	Identify what you fear. Build a risk analysis around it actually happening.

Application # 4

Know When to Fold 'Em

Level II

For most people, the issue of when to "let go" is the most difficult. There are two sides to this issue.

There are those for whom letting go is easy. Their pattern is to find that critical moment when it becomes uncomfortable, too uncomfortable, and then throw in the towel rather than figure out their responsibility in what is not working. These people usually have a fall-back position already identified before things get too "hot". Generally they have a rather large fear that others will find them out. They think of themselves as 'imposters'.

The problem with this particular pattern is that while it probably moves the person through the critical moment in an easier fashion, there is usually a price to pay, sometimes large, and often at the time of life when people should be reaping the rewards for their earlier years. The consequences might include unfinished business, unlearned lessons, lack of completion and often a trail of broken commitments. The consequences to these things are often a lack of credibility, a lack of preparation for more difficult situations, and a lack of followers in critical moments.

The other side of this issue is hanging on too long. How does one determine the moment when it is time to let go?

Objective:

- Clear understanding of when a cycle needs to be broken in order to create more Grace in the larger patterns of your life.
- To become better at assessing the realities of risk and applying that knowledge to tough decisions.

Prepare:

Define Your Initiative:

Identify a situation which has caused you a repetitive sense of frustration and anxiety. (Remember, a person who is living Grace would not have this ongoing situation.)

Write a brief description of what you will work on in your journal!

The Challenge: With any situation involving the decision to let go and move on, the challenge is always twofold. First, you must understand clearly what the lesson is that must be learned. Second, you must have the courage to stay or go, depending on the answer. Making the decision is hard, but executing the decision is often *as* hard as or even harder than you expected.

The Skill Set: There are multiple skills involved in the resolution of a "fold em" concern. Here are some of the more important ones:

- Knowing your own patterns is an advanced skill set. Being able to identify them in an emotional situation around 'letting go' is even more advanced.
- If the issue is lack of completion, you must be able to identify what you need to complete before you can move on. It is very easy to pick the wrong thing. Sometimes you simply need to prove your worth. Other times you need to resolve a relationship. Sometimes, there is the obligation to finish what you started.
- Communicating without anger or judgment is an important capability accompanying a decision to let go. The more invested you were in the situation, the more difficult this is to achieve.
- Staying clear when confronted with "push back" for your decision is another required skill. Not letting others manipulate your thoughts is difficult in these situations or you would have had more clarity about the decision in the first place.

Approach

The answers, as always, lie within the five-step process and the three fundamentals of Grace. Finding Clarity, Confidence, and Trust within each of the five-steps will help you to make and execute your decisions around the issue you have surfaced.

Examine the five-step process:

Critical Moment: What is the nature of the critical moment that caused you to examine this issue in the first place? What are your feelings and what fears do you have around this situation?

Vision: Identify the ideal outcome. The ideal should *not* include a willful hanging on but instead the feelings and sense of release that should come from successful (Graceful) resolution. (Not hanging on is very difficult for most people.)

Be sure to look for the possible pattern in this circumstance by comparing it to other situations from your life. If you find a pattern, identify the fear underlying the pattern.

Assessment: Identify your options and assess the risks. This work must be done carefully. Remember, you are probably emotional about this or it would not be an issue.

Engagement: Make a decision based on what you "know" to be right. Do not base your decision on the easier path.

Execution: As you execute your decision check your results. Be careful to separate emotional reactions from objective analysis.

Outcomes:

What Should Happen: The decision to let go should be about completion. You should feel as though you have completed what you set out to do *or* that you have completed what you are capable of doing within that situation. You should know the difference between a cop-out and the true sense of futility or damage that will occur should you stay.

What Can Go Wrong: If you leave too early, or before understanding the nature of the lesson, you will manifest the same lesson again. You will find yourself confronting similar situations with similar feelings in your future. On the other hand, if you stay too long, the situation will become worse with fewer options for a successful exit. Your resources will be further depleted as you avoid the decision you still ultimately need to make. Finally, you may make a decision and then be haunted by a sense of making the wrong decision.

How to Fix It: Revisit what you are feeling, and why, to determine if you accurately described the feeling and fear the situation provoked initially. Within those feelings or fears will be the understandings you need to readdress the situation. This is *Level II* work, so start with the assumption that if it were easy it would be marked as such. Objectivity is the starting place for solving problems. Emotions *will* cloud the issue.

Advanced Intelligence:

Situations where you long to escape always represent important life lessons. You must acknowledge and work with the reality that you created this situation in order to reach a successful (Grace filled) conclusion. Asking and understanding why you manifested the situation in the first place is critical to arriving at the correct response.

Fear is what causes us to hold onto what is only *partly* right. Knowing the right moment to hold on and work harder and when to let go is a finely tuned balance that starts with the assumption that the Universe wants you to be happy. If you can work through all of the guilt and uncertainty about the unknown, the answer to when to "hold 'em" and when to "fold 'em" is usually apparent. If you are clear in your mind that the situation is unlikely to improve no matter how much effort you put in, then it is time to go. Trust the Universe, and put yourself in a situation in which hope can once again enter the picture.

Here are some possible issues and solutions you may find helpful:

Issues	Possible Underlying Causes	Possible Pathways to Grace
You have failed at this particular venture before and you hesitate to let go again.	• Fear of failure. • Fear of making a mistake. • Fear of what others will think.	Differentiate the fears and feelings in this situation from previous situations. Do not judge this situation based on other situations. If there is a common issue, you will find it, but it still needs to be solved around *this* situation.
You are unable to make this situation black and white, and as a result, you remain confused about your course of action. This causes you to make no decision.	• Inability to handle conflict. • Avoidance. • Lack of clarity about your real needs. • Not yet understanding the real issue underlying your discomfort.	• Review priorities in your life when analyzing risk. Stack those against your fear of conflict and get on with it. • Look again at why it is wrong and see if there is another underlying issue, which when surfaced, will clarify the situation.
You're frozen, unable to make a decision.	• Too easily influenced by others. • Guilt.	Prioritize your own needs. Do not allow others to push you into actions you will regret, whether you choose to stay or leave.

Issues	Possible Underlying Causes	Possible Pathways to Grace
Guilt.	Training, manipulation by others.	Separate the guilt from the decision. Get therapy for the guilt and get on with the decision.
Staying when you know you have to go.	• Still hanging onto the potential rather than dealing with the reality. Hanging on to hope that it will change. • Fear of the unknown.	Evaluate risks more carefully. What are the risks involved in staying and in going? What is the potential for change in this situation vs the fantasy? Determine how much of your inability to act is fear of unknown.
Going too soon.	Fear of failing, lack of self confidence, inability to confront inadequacies.	Be more honest with yourself. Ask for help. Address the issue of too much pride. Allow yourself to be imperfect.

Issue	Possible Underlying Cause	Possible Path back to Grace
Getting hyper, or louder, or more chatty, because you are trying to get someone's attention.	Trying to help control and form the other person's opinion of you rather than *allowing* them to discover you more naturally.	Do you feel as though this might be your only opportunity to get the person to notice you? Trust that the Universe will cause them to notice you if it is important. Otherwise, you may be forming a negative impression which is worse than none at all.
Trying to act or look smart for someone's benefit.	Possible sense that your future, career or potential relationship might depend on this person believing you are smart.	Pay attention to what really advances your life, career or relationships along. Realize that if you are meant to have a relationship with this person, it will evolve of its own accord. This is an issue of Trust.

Application #6

Self Containment

Level II

Here's a fun thought. One of the definitions of containment is "a structure or system designed to prevent the accidental release of radioactive materials from a reactor". Do you know what makes you radioactive? Do you have clarity regarding those hidden issues that cause you to "lose it"?

Think of being self-contained as a demeanor evident of having prevented the destructive reactions you have when someone hits your button. (You may be destructive internally as well as externally; fuming is still a reaction.) Try to think of the quicksilver, spasmodic, erratic and sometimes unpredictable reactions you may only be subliminally aware of. Becoming self-contained allows you to both curb these reactions and find a way to be peaceful when someone intentionally or inadvertently steps on you.

Objective:

1. To no longer have a negative reaction to the things which consistently disturb you. This is not easy. Do not underestimate how deeply you hold the beliefs that drive your trigger points.
2. To remain 'above' the behaviors of others and to maintain a clear, confident and trusting attitude, regardless of others' choices.
3. To understand (in the moment) that others' behaviors are about them, not about you. (Obviously, this application is a *Level II* for a reason!)

Prepare:

Define Your Initiative: What triggers your anger *every* time? *Everyone* has a hot spot. Do you react to people being disrespectful? Do you react to people being lazy? Are you completely annoyed when someone makes fun of how serious you are? Spend some time and find one of your triggers to work on. Remember, this is Level II. Do not expect to become "contained" in a few moves.

Write a brief description of what you will work on in your journal!

The Challenge: The biggest challenge you will encounter in your radioactive responses is the tendency to take the other person's behavior personally. Maturity and evolution in Grace will lead you to see others' behavior as a reflection of their own fear. When you can see that the behavior of others is not about you, you will be freer to assess and deal with your own reaction separately.

The Skill Set: Being able to control your internal responses in the moment and give yourself time to work through the process is a very sophisticated skill. You must be able to stay aware of your reaction, recognize the critical moment and not react. If you are able to do this, you have a greater chance of getting to a more positive place, without doing damage to yourself or others in the process.

Approach:

It will be very important for you to realize how much judgment you hold regarding your triggers. Usually, the triggers for your radioactive reactions are buried deeply under something that looks like a principle or a value. However, it is usually a very large insecurity. The more self-contained you are regarding most issues, the more surprising it is when one sets you off.

Examine the five-step process:

Critical Moment: Examine your feelings carefully and attempt to identify the root of the reaction. You may perceive fear or anger to be the feeling, but what is the value or principle that the other person or situation has violated?

Vision: You will want to imagine a situation in which this same set of circumstances causes *no* reaction in you. This will be very difficult. Achieving a state of peace may make you feel as though you are betraying your sense of self or your values. For example, suppose you believe that someone is treating you unfairly. This exercise is asking you to have no reaction or to be detached from their behavior. Remember that Grace is a state of being 'above it'. Being detached does not mean that you do not care. It means you can remain unemotional when something or someone finds your trigger point.

Assessment: As you analyze the risks of letting this issue go (or not making it into a big deal), you will want to carefully review your history for the consequences of holding on to it.

- Has your response to the issue served you well? Has it caused you to consistently respond in ways that make your life more difficult?
- Have you made the world a better place because of your reactions?
- Have your crusades actually been effective? At what cost?
- Have you been openly curious about what caused the situation in the first place? Openly curious means that you have suspended judgment or criticism in order to understand why the situation unfolded as it did. It means that you are trusting that others involved are also on a journey and have blind spots just as you do. It means you understand that each person is a reflection of their beliefs and upbringing and not everyone shares your same understanding of how things *should* be done.

Engagement in this situation should be a decision to gain understanding. There are two paths that you may pursue:

- External: If you engage with the event or person in a non-judgmental, curious way you may come to understand what caused the event or behavior that triggered your reaction. Asking questions (without bias) and being open to the response are necessary to this step. Gathering information helps you understand how you may have triggered another person's fears and thereby set off the behavior in the first place.
- Internal: If you do not have the opportunity to actually pursue understanding interactively you can do this work intuitively. You will want to *become* the other person in order to identify what caused him or her to act in that specific way. You cannot do this step by asking what would cause you to behave in that way. You are a different

person!

Execute: If you are able to deal with your own fears, you can now attempt to interact with the event or individuals differently. Try to respond in a way that is open, confident and removed (detached). If you find you are not operating in an open, confident and removed mode during the interaction, go back to the beginning of the cycle of steps and do it again, this time incorporating whatever you are learning about yourself.

Outcomes:

What Should Happen: The next time you encounter a situation or a behavior that has always triggered a response from you, you will be much more objective. Your new reaction to the situation will be Graceful. This exercise teaches acceptance and ease in dealing with upsetting circumstances.

What Can Go Wrong:

- The other person does not know (or acknowledge) that he or she is doing the things that cause you to react. Even when you attempt to discuss the issues, he or she closes down and denies that your feelings and reactions are valid. This can cause you to close down as well.
- You have formed such an intense dislike for the other person and his or her behavior that you cannot let go of your sense of how bad or wrong he or she is. This is communicated by you as an air of superiority. Things do not improve.
- You fail to identify the issue as your problem and continue to blame the other person or the situation as unfair or unstable.

How to Fix It: This is a very intense and often lengthy process. Each time you fall off the tightrope of Grace, you will want to go back to step 1 and 2 of the cycle. Return to looking for the real fear behind your reaction and continue to evolve your vision to include having *no* reaction to this particular trigger. Continue to look for understanding, not judgment, of the circumstance.

When a person violates a value or a principle, do not assume that the person is therefore evil or bad. Assume a giant fear. Be curious and respectful about what that person is afraid of and you may find your own means to resolve the issue. This does not mean that you leave yourself open to being hurt by the misunderstandings and misbehavior of others. It means that you are compassionate toward their fears and the experiences that caused them.

Advanced Intelligence:
You may believe strongly that your reactions are coming from a place of right. Any time you are having an intense emotional reaction to someone else's choice, you are acting from a fear that you may not have identified and managed. Whenever you find yourself in a situation that triggers your nuclear reaction, the situation or person is acting as a mirror. Assume the purpose of this mirror is to teach you something that is going on inside of you and moving you away from Grace. The situation or the person is, in fact, a gift.

Some possible issues and pathways:

Issues	Possible Causes	Possible Corrections
The other person discounts your intelligence.	He or she feels that you do not respect them.	Identify if you are sending them a message of disrespect that is triggering the other person's behavior. Imagine what it is like to deal with *you*.

Issues	Possible Causes	Possible Corrections
Unfairness.	Need to control others' behavior in a manner that fits with your *sense* of right. (This is a naive view that focuses on the micro instead of the macro).	Look at the situation with a more macro view. Assume the ultimate fairness of the Universe and identify how this unfairness fits in with the law of cause and affect. How is it helping you learn *your* lessons? (Assume that other people will get their lessons in their own way over an indefinite period of time).

Issues	Possible Causes	Possible Corrections
Others not listening or paying attention when you are trying to explain something.	1. You are being disrespectful of them or their time in your neediness. 2. You are over-explaining. 3. You are internally convinced that inattentiveness is saying something about your value.	4. Check your timing; is it appropriate? 5. Identify your fear and determine if it is coming from your own lack of confidence. 6. Watch the other's behavior more carefully. Is the other person consistently inattentive in the same way with others?

Issues	Possible Causes	Possible Corrections
The other person interrupts you or cuts you off as if you are irrelevant.	7. You are trying too hard to impress or gain a favorable opinion from this person. He or she makes you feel insecure. 8. The other person is not doing it to hurt you. He or she is simply not focused.	• Identify if you are being over-responsive to this person. • See if you can find the fear behind your choice to be super-sensitive. • Examine your relationship with this person. Are you close enough to talk about it?
Others seem to advance when you deserve it more.	You are attempting to devise your life's progression based on others' expectations rather than having a strong sense of your own journey.	Spend time with a more complete vision of your destiny and assess whether you have stepped onto the wrong path in order to prove something. Trust more in the timing of the Universe.

Issues	Possible Causes	Possible Corrections
Others jump to incorrect conclusions regarding your motives.	They are looking at you through their own beliefs. It is a natural and expected response. Your issue is that you take it personally.	If you were totally confident, would you care so much? Spend some time thinking about why it is so important to you that others understand you better. Recognize that this reaction is a manifestation of you judging your worth through the eyes of others. Confident people respond calmly, regardless of judgments by others.
Incessant teasing.	The other person is trying to get your attention and doesn't know any better. You have a big reaction to it which causes the other person to push even harder.	Identify the reason your reaction is so intense. Treat it like a boundary issue. Remember, when you indicate your preferences for a boundary you must first let go of your negative judgment of the other person if it is to work.

CLARITY

Application #7

Better Communication in Tough Circumstances

When you are angry or emotional, you are potentially responding to the wrong things. You are going to assume another person's motives for doing something are to harm you. Until you are able to set aside your emotions and find out the real facts, you will react to the current situation based on its similarity to something which may have happened in your past.

Objective:

- To remain cool-headed and effective while gathering the truth in a situation that affects you emotionally.
- To find compassion and understanding for the other person even while they are doing something that would normally offend you intensely.

Prepare:

Define Your Initiative: Choose any situation where another person has done something which offends you intensely.

Write a brief description of what you will work on in your journal!

The Challenge: Staying objective will be your biggest challenge. While you believe you already know why the other person did what they did, you really do not. The more locked in and rigid you are, the more stuck you will be as you attempt to work toward a better conclusion.

The Skill Set: First, you make the decision to look for more information. The skill you want to develop is in how you do it. Because directness is not the norm, others may find it unnerving that you are trying to understand what happened. You will need to be open, curious and non-defensive as you gather information. This is difficult to pull off if you are still feeling angry or upset.

Approach:

It is important to remember that your objective is Grace. You are looking for an effortless flow in your responses to the reality of your life. Start with the assumption that you do not understand what is happening rather than the assumption that someone has just done you wrong. (Have you ever reacted and then found out that you were all wrong? The goal is to wait and react *after* confirming whether or not you are right.)

Examine the five-step process:

Critical Moment: In response to the other person's choice, identify what you are feeling and why. Look for the long-term pattern that might be represented (see Application #6).

Vision: Envision an outcome where you are clear on what drove the other person's action. Assume that it is not about you, but something in the other person's make-up which is driving his or her behaviors. See yourself letting go of your initial reaction and moving into a more comfortable place.

Assessment: Carefully analyze the risk of staying in and reacting from your current mode versus slowing down and gathering more information before you proceed.

Engage the other person in a dialogue in which you help them clarify what was intended by their actions vs. what occurred. Do not be afraid to ask directly what motivated the person's actions. (Note: even if the person does not respond truthfully, he or she is highly likely to be more careful in the future.)

Execution: Together, identify what choices you will make in the future. Watch to see what choices they make going forward. Stay clear on what you have learned.

Outcomes:

What Should Happen: Ideally, when you slow down and seek more information, you will help the other person understand the impact and consequences of his or her choices. When confronted with the results of bad choices, others usually are remorseful and often make a commitment not to repeat them. You may also find that their behavior was motivated more by their fear than it was by trying to do you damage. Even if they intended you harm, it was still rooted in their fear.

What Can Go Wrong:

- You shift from trying to be curious into a state of attempting to prove your point and how the other person has wronged you.
- The other person is in denial and accuses you of being paranoid.
- The other person diverts the conversation to accusing you of everything you have done wrong in the relationship.

How to Fix It:

- You will need to stay very clear about what you feel and why and not engage in explanations. If you begin to argue over what really happened you will regret your attempt to find out what was really going on. Regain the momentum by asking rather than explaining. Remember that the overall approach to this problem is to gain understanding.
- If you are treated as though you are overreacting, repeat how the behavior made you feel and do not debate what occurred.
- The very thing which offends you in another's behavior may be something that you are not only quite capable of doing, but may even do regularly. Obviously you are unaware of it. Describe the behavior you dislike in one sentence and ask others if they've observed you doing it.

Advanced Intelligence:

If you choose to ask the other person what they intended, they do not have to tell the absolute truth for you to get the result you seek. You are trying to get the behavior to stop. The very act of talking with the person to determine their intent and clarify your own assumptions is often enough for them realize that they are not invisible. Your open reaction with no attempt to control the other person or get even is often so unexpected that it will cause the other person to pause the next time they attempt to do damage.

The following chart contains some of the issues and responses that often occur with this type of issue:

Issue	Possible Cause	Possible Path to Grace
The person attempts to go around you when they should be asking your permission for something.	• They are afraid you will say "no". • They do not respect you so they see no need to ask.	Assume that you do not know which of the two causes it is. A powerful response (confident, clear, and trusting) is to go to the person and ask if the behavior is motivated by one of the two possible causes.
Remember the executive who found her peers were meeting with her subordinates in an earlier chapter?	• They perceived her to be too confident to need to be informed of each and every encounter with her team. • They were trying to be divisive.	A very powerful response might have been to go to her peers and innocently ask them what they were intending and why they had not trusted her enough to come to her first.

Issue	Possible Cause	Possible Path to Grace
Someone does something which negatively affects your ability to accomplish some goal.	• He or she intended to annoy you. • He or she had no idea of the impact the behavior had on your plans.	The second option is much more likely. You will not know until you ask the person if he or she understood how his or her choices would affect you.

Application #8

Level II

Telling the Truth When Doing So Is Uncomfortable.

Too often, our life is complicated by situations which we could have diffused or diminished through honesty. Sometimes we even know that situations are building momentum as potential crises and yet we still choose not to confront the problems. Why? To deal with the situation we are going to have to tell someone the truth. In the telling of that truth, we are certain to set off a chain of events that will potentially change the very fabric of our lives.

Objective:

- To find a comfort level in communicating difficult topics more honestly.
- To learn that Honesty is more effective in creating Peace than avoidance.

Prepare:

Define Your Initiative: How much value you take away from this application is up to you. Remember that this is a *Level II* exercise and you are going to address a communication opportunity which you may have been avoiding. Choose any situation where another person may be operating with an inaccurate understanding of how you feel because it has been too difficult a topic area for you to deal with directly.

Write a brief description of what you will work on in your journal!

The Challenge: The challenge is to communicate differently than you have in the past if you want a different response. Do not assume that you have not been heard. Instead, assume that you have not been clear or that the other person is so invested in denial that he or she refuses to listen.

123

Too often, the person who has been holding back has done so because he or she is accepting the other person's need for deception is more relevant than his or her own need for Truth in the relationship. If you find yourself sabotaging your own needs for a truthful life, you are accepting a form of slavery. The other person, in his or her own fear of the truth, is making you a victim to his or her fear. Your behaviors become distorted in your efforts not to say anything which will cause the other person to have a negative reaction to your words.

The Skill Set: Communicating honestly requires some very specific techniques which you may not have tried in past dialogues. The following sequence of steps is usually very effective if done without being emotional or judgmental of the other person:

- State what you are feeling and why.
- State why you believe the situation is occurring (your assumptions, your guesses, etc.).
- Ask the other person if they agree with why you think it is happening and if not, what their perception is.
- If the other person believes your assumptions to be incorrect you may allow that to pass but reiterate your feelings (others cannot disagree with what you feel).
- If you have already decided what action steps you will take, state them. If you want to decide the steps together, start that dialogue now.

Approach:

You will need to address two problems as you work through this issue. First, you must understand why you have not communicated honestly up until now. Often these situations are the cumulative affect of numerous defaults in honest communication because of some fear you have about what will happen if you tell the truth.

Second, you must become clear about the actions that should be taken now that you are being more open. You should not consider having an honest communication about a difficult subject unless you are also prepared to change the reality that made the situation occur.

124

Examine the five-step process:

Critical Moment: If you are holding back on feeling or being clear in your life in any way, and if you feel the repercussions from that lack of clarity, you must see this as a moment that can have life changing implications. Identify what you are feeling and why as a preliminary step to this communication.

Vision: Create a very distinct vision of what you would like to have happen if you communicate what you are feeling and it goes perfectly. What is perfection? This is a complicated step and might need to be done in phases. For example, perhaps you are getting ready to tell a subordinate that he or she is not performing up to standard. What do you want to happen? What does success look like? Perhaps this is a relationship issue. What is your vision? Is your desire to be out of the relationship, change the relationship or create a process for changing it?

Assessment: As you analyze the risks, be sure to hold yourself accountable for wanting things both ways. For example, in a relationship that is not working, you may want your freedom but not want to be alone or to have the pain of completing the one you are in. Communicating your feelings will probably set off a chain of events you may not feel ready for.

Challenge yourself to understand where your weaknesses lie. You can pretend that your reluctance to communicate honestly is about the other person but that perspective most certainly lacks clarity. It is probably the fear of opening this Pandora's Box that is holding you in place.

In this application, Engagement has two stages. First stage is the decision-making. Decide what you will do and how you will communicate your decisions. Second stage is the actual engagement with the other person. Overcome your dread and have the dialogue. In this second stage, you may want to revisit the five-step cycle together to determine what your options and choices are for going forward (unless you have already made those decisions as well).
Execution: Once you've said the things you wish to say and have articulated the decisions that go with saying those things, you must then be attentive to what occurs. Are you or the others involved following through

with the next steps? It is quite common to find yourself back in the same "do" loop after having steeled yourself for the tough interaction. People will often act as though nothing has happened. People are invested in the false premise under which things were operating in the first place. If nothing changes, go back to the beginning and reevaluate where you lacked the commitment to follow through.

Execution is an intricate dance where emotional barriers are complicated and layered like an onion. As you begin to address the action steps that arise from dealing with a problem more authentically, you may come to think that communicating the truth was the easiest step to take. Executing the necessary actions to reach a more real state of existence will remind you why you did not step up to the plate sooner.

Outcomes:

What Should Happen: As you tackle the difficult conversations with clear-headed bravery, you should find that your life becomes less complicated and less confusing. Each conversation should make it simpler to maneuver through what was previously a maze of difficult choices. Starting the process is scary and intimidating. If you have not been honest for a long time, the journey will take a while. As you make honest communication a part of your life it will take on a Grace that others will envy. You will learn to value honesty above the escapes you sought previously through avoidance.

What Can Go Wrong: The other person tells you that you are wrong or attempts to manipulate you into thinking that your feelings are mistaken. This is a very difficult thing to deal with when the other person is able to make you feel guilt when you should be feeling release.

How to Fix It: Always express what is true for you in terms of your feelings. While people can argue endlessly with you about your conclusions or your facts, no one can tell you that your feelings are wrong. (See 'The Skill Set')

126

Advanced Intelligence:

Honest communication is more than a dialogue; it is a way of being. An honest communicator is also able to see the steps that must be taken as a result of the honesty. A person who chooses to communicate honestly also chooses to be responsible for what they must *do* as a result of expressing true feelings on difficult subjects. If you are fortunate enough to observe someone who is good at being clear and truthful you may, at first, think that they have a lot of luck and opportunity in their life. If you look closer you'll see a person who is available for that luck because they have not allowed dishonest situations to complicate their ability to act when opportunity occurs. While fraught with risks, honesty is the foundation for a vital and ultimately Graceful life.

Communicating honestly is a Level II exercise because truthfulness creates an obligation and responsibility to live an authentic life. You must not only find a way to say what you feel, but to be prepared to follow through and address the situation with your actions. (If you are honest, but don't follow through, you will simply be offensive).Only the very brave live their lives with this kind of clarity. You cannot make the other person responsible for the next steps. You must be ready to take them with or without the other person's cooperation. It is, after all, *your* truth. You must also become clear about why you have chosen not to be clear up to now. What are you afraid of losing if they do take you seriously?

The following table offers some ideas for handling issues requiring honest communication:

Issues	Possible Causes	Possible Paths back to Grace
The other person will have a melt-down if you try to be honest.	This person has learned that this is a way to distract you.	Tell the person that you find this discussion very hard and that you would really like him or her to support you as you attempt to be truthful.
The other person goes on as if you have said nothing.	The person thinks that if he or she ignores you, what you're saying is not true. At the very least, the person does not have to deal with you if they pretend you have not said a thing.	Try to get the person to problem solve with you. If he or she is incapable, then you must identify what you have control over and tell the person what *you* will do.
The other person argues with you about the correctness of your conclusions or feelings.	If the person can prove you wrong, then nothing will have to change.	*Do not argue.* If the discussion starts to become an argument, simply restate your feelings and indicate that the fact that you feel that way means that the situation has to change. Take action.

Application #9

Understanding "to Manifest"

People who are working to master the concept of Grace under fire, have an understanding of cause and effect that is often elusive to those whose lives are out of control. These rare individuals understand that their reality is a manifestation (evidence) of their will, choices and destiny. Absolutely *everything* in their lives, good and bad, is a form of divine disclosure of their purpose.

How can you use this concept? Even if you do not believe it or would like to argue its truth, step back and pretend for a moment that there is a purpose, created or manifested by you, for every single circumstance in your life. The fact that you exist in this moment, with this set of circumstances, is a reflection of choices you have made, knowingly or unknowingly. Suppose that these choices were deliberate. Suppose, at some unconscious level, you knew exactly what you were doing when you went to work for this monster, placed yourself in the path of this storm, or brought this impossible situation into your life.

Why bother to think in this way? What does it give you in terms of creating more Grace in your responses? Assuming you created the situation gives you control. Even if the idea that you manifest everything is totally fictitious, imagine the empowerment it gives you in situations where you feel like a victim. Suddenly there is a problem solving path that you might never have pursued. As a result, you are able to find direction rather than falling into your emotions.

If you want something more concrete, think of this as a way of determining the cause and effect relationships in your reality. Choose an effect (your current dilemma). Trace all of the steps, choices and events backwards until you find a cause. Often the 'cause' will present more appropriate choices for now.

Objective:

- To gain control over events in your life by accepting that you created them.
- To better understand the laws of cause and effect and how they are operating in your life.
- To completely reject the concept of being a victim of circumstance.
- To more completely own and respond to the situations which affect the long-term quality of your life.

Prepare:

Define Your Initiative: Identify something in your life that is causing you grief. Pick something that is causing you way too much trouble. It might be a relationship, a project or a situation. It might be wise to start with something that you would not necessarily define as *huge*. You can always work up to huge...

Write a brief description of what you will work on in your journal!

The Challenge: You will need to accept that you have a blind spot and you will need to act as though you cannot see clearly around this situation. This is a big challenge for the ego, particularly if you pride yourself on being a pretty "together" personality.

The Skill Set: You must build your ability to quickly identify why and how you manifest a situation and what you should do with it. This is an analytical skills set and you will want to practice looking at any situation to determine if you can find the cause and effect relationship. At first, try looking at situations of others where it is easier to be objective. You will get much better at this particular skill the more you practice.

Approach:

Assume that this situation is evidence of self-knowledge which you need to gain in order to live more Gracefully. As you work with the five-steps of the cycle and the three fundamentals of Grace, you are attempting to find clarity about this situation's larger purpose in your life. You will want to determine how your personality is the cause of, or is affected by, this problem. What makes this circumstance so challenging for *you*? How does it reflect a pattern in your journey? What does the solution to this particular issue represent on a larger scale in your life?

Clearly, we are challenging you to a higher level of understanding than we have demanded in previous applications. This level of understanding could be applied to any of the previous situations you have examined. Because this may be a new approach, the following example is offered for your review.

> Example: Suppose you have a dog which is turning mean. You love the dog but it has become a liability. In this example, your dog has just attacked a very small (five pound) dog for no apparent reason. The little dog survives, barely, after three surgeries.

We will work through this example in a way which reflects Grace.

Apply the 5 step process to your issue. Review the evolution of the story of the dog for examples of how to look for your personal challenges and manifestations within a situation to help determine the path to Grace.

Examine the five-step process:

Critical Moment: Assume that whatever you have chosen represents a critical (potentially life changing) moment in your journey. Identify what you are feeling about the situation and why you are feeling it. When you ask "Why?" assume that the answer is that you are feeling what you are feeling because you need to break a pattern, learn something about yourself or redirect your path to a lighter, more effortless flow.

Example: You brought the situation into your life. No, you did not order your dog to attack the small dog, but you have a situation in which an animal for which you are responsible did something completely out of control. You might be feeling confused, scared, worried about the potential consequences (will the owner of the small dog expect me to pay for the surgeries?), etc. Get clear on your fears as the first step.

Vision: As you create a vision for what you would like to have happen. Try to focus this vision on a greater understanding of why you have created this reality and what you are trying to learn. Get a sense of how you would like to respond. Also, think in terms of resolving this situation to create a more peaceful, flowing life *in your future* as opposed to an easier immediate path. This approach is an evolution in your understanding of achieving Grace as a way of life.

Example: Your vision might be that you wish to understand the implications of this event in your life so you can make the perfect decision for the dog and for you. (An alternate, more common response would be to wish or assume that the dog gets over its craziness and turns into a loving and predictable animal. This is an escapist vision and not the vision a person seeking Grace would develop).

Assessment: As you look for the facts, stay completely clear about what this situation means in terms of the risks. You will want to understand what those risks may mean to you. Determine the potential for future problems and how your feelings can confuse your sense of clarity in the situation. Remember to assume that you created this situation to teach yourself something about you.

Example: You are aware that your dog does not have the appropriate behaviors for a domestic pet. You think about what that means long-term and short-term. What are the potential risks involved in maintaining an animal that has clearly shown it is not a good fit as a pet? What does her behavior indicate in terms of how she needs to be handled now as opposed to how you have handled her previously?

How prepared are you to make changes to your own care and handling of this dog based on her behavior? What is it about you that this situation may help you to understand? As an outsider this may seem very obvious, but when any of us face similar issues, this kind of objectivity is elusive.

You might recognize that you *want* to pretend that things will return to the way they were before the dog attacked. Instead, you look at the larger pattern and realize that you have been in similar situations with similar implications. Before, your choice has often been to pretend that things will get better without any change in your behavior. You review your history and realize that they rarely have.

As a result, you look squarely at the risks and choices involved. You gather information and statistics regarding dogs attacking domestic pets. You identify and face what might be the worst possible outcome. Worst case, the dog becomes increasingly violent and you end up with a terrible liability that you might avoid by acting now.

Engagement: This is the stage in the cycle where you wrestle with the actual choices. You make a decision. Think about the past patterns that you examined in the analysis phase and use those to help you make the decision in this situation. These patterns contribute to your clarity. Try not to make your decision based on what others may think or tell you because they do not share your unique history. Make your decision based on your own patterns and what this situation represents. Go against the natural inclinations that have caused you to take an easier path in the past.

133

> Example: You decide that the dog is not a pet. Rather than deny this reality, you decide to approach the life of the dog differently than you have in the past. This dog must be confined. You decide to treat the dog as a watch dog rather than a pet who is involved in all facets of your life. This is a difficult decision for you. It is not what you had in mind for the dog initially and it is sometimes hard to let go.

Execution: Because this situation reflects some not-so-successful life tendencies, you realize that being consistent in your execution will be difficult. You will be inclined to slip into old behaviors and belief patterns. You must commit to yourself that you will pay attention to critical moments more diligently in order to catch yourself sooner.

Outcomes:

What Should Happen: If you acknowledge how and why you manifested this problem, your clarity will help you deal with this issue (and others) more effectively. The stress of the situation should diminish and you should find that your life, both in this situation and elsewhere, begins to flow in new ways.

What Can Go Wrong: You may fail to recognize that if this is, in fact, a life pattern. You may lose your focus and allow the patterns and old behaviors to reassert themselves. The problem will come back or you will create new ones which are similar.

How to Fix It: Begin with the understanding that this is a recovery process and not just "solving a problem." As such, you will need to develop your own 'twelve step process" in order to catch yourself and prevent the return of old patterns. You may need to build a support structure once you realize this is a larger issue than it initially seemed.

Advanced Intelligence:

All critical situations can be approached in this way. You can change the quality of your life as well as resolve the issues at hand more successfully. Assume that you "manifest" all that happens in order to address your own life patterns. Look for the larger pattern in any difficult situation, and your solutions will be more lasting and more satisfying.

Determining how you manifest difficult situations in your life may feel punitive when you start working with it as a concept. You may see things in yourself you do not want to see. Assuming you manifested a bad situation may reveal potentially dark sides of your personality. While upsetting, it is more liberating than just reacting to a circumstance in your life. By examining the situation as a potential pattern, you may find and resolve larger, more pervasive issues in your life.

Issue	Possible Cause	Possible Path to Grace
Denial; ostrich behavior.	Fear of confronting the decisions it will take to get back on track. Laziness.	Take a clearer look at the long-term risks of *not* acting now. It may make the now seem easier than it did before.
Fear of losing control.	To respond appropriately, you need to let go in some way that scares you. This causes you to revert quickly to the very behaviors that have not worked in the past.	Take it in smaller bites. Find a way to break down your response into little, manageable pieces.
Fear of denying others something they want.	Inability to set boundaries out of a need to please others.	Become clearer on who pays the consequences when others' demands put you in a bad situation. If the risk to them is minimal and the risk to you is high, get clear on who pays and what their approval is really worth to you.

Application # 10

Level II

Cause and Effect as a Means for Coping with Serious Crisis

There exists in almost everyone's journey that one event or situation that becomes our "before and after". Life is somehow different after this moment and we are faced with a division in our lives that makes us whole or tears us apart. If you think of this event as your personal test, your personal challenge, and quite possibly, your own personal creation, you may find that your choices regarding it take on more meaning and a greater sense of direction.

Objective:

- To assume a purpose in each and every event.
- To trust in a larger plan or order.
- To make peace with the crises in your life.

Prepare:

Define Your Initiative: This application is for that "bigger than life" moment when something goes irrevocably wrong. Perhaps you've been fired, lost your home, are going through a divorce, have lost a loved one, were involved in a serious accident, or are suddenly faced with a health crisis. No matter what you choose to address in this application, it should be something that has or will change the fabric of your being and forever cause you look at life differently.

If you've been fortunate enough not to experience one of these moments, try looking at a life-changing event in another person's life to begin understanding the process. You will not necessarily want to share your observations with that person because they may not yet be ready to hear what you discover.

<u>**Write a brief description of what you will work on in your journal!**</u>

The Challenge: The two most negative responses to crisis are to become cynical or to take on a victim mentality. Either response will take you away from Grace. Whether or not to indulge in one of these two responses is your choice. Unfortunately, to either become cynical or victimized is an easy trap which carries the long-term potential of producing either an angry, bitter person, or even worse, a lifeless one with no vitality.

The Skill Set: Ideally, the larger crisis will challenge your deductive skills and impact your ability to manage any ambiguous situation. For example, if you manifested this cancer, what caused you to manifest this particular cancer in this particular location and at this particular time? What is the symbolism of this crisis? The better you become at identifying the symbolic path to a crisis, the more apparent your best response may become.

For example, suppose you have breast cancer. Is it possible that you have done a lousy job of nurturing yourself over time? Perhaps you expend a lot of energy nurturing others while neglecting yourself. The obvious path is the medical path and putting yourself in the hands of the "experts". With the medical path in the hands of others, sometimes a simultaneous fight around the symbolism of the cancer and its possible connection to a larger purpose is quite rewarding. Choosing a personal response to the disease can also create a sense of engagement (rather than helplessness) while you are being treated medically.

Approach:

Assume that this situation was meant to be in your life. Realize that you have everything you need to proceed. Your main intention is to proceed with Grace.

Begin by examining the choices that led to this moment. You should soon see that somehow you had no real choice. Events leading up to the current situation will seem orchestrated.

For example you may have found that things kept happening to bring you

138

to this point of crisis. You were moving toward this situation like an actor moving around the stage with a particular spot at a particular moment in the play as your destination. Assume, for the moment, the inevitability of this situation and let go of the "what ifs?" They are useless to you now and only make the journey harder.

Examine the five-step process:

Critical Moment: As you identify your feelings about this situation, also ask yourself what it means in your life. Why would you manifest such a thing? How do you respond if the experience is to add meaning and richness to who you are and who you are becoming? Clearly this is a critical moment. What is the symbolism in your life's journey?

Vision: Remember, you seek an outcome which teaches you what you have to learn and helps you evolve where you need to evolve. Include in your vision the wish to absorb this crisis in your life with Confidence, Clarity about its true meaning, and Trust that you are exactly where you are supposed to be.

When you first learn to create your visions, you are most likely to develop easy and simple outcomes that reflect your *desires*. As you mature, you will seek elegant pathways that reflect your *potential*.

Assessment: As you assess your situation, your greatest risk is in resisting reality instead of embracing it. Resisting the opportunity that is offered to you is a waste of energy. This is your reality to deal with; you have arrived here for a reason and you want to integrate this moment into your evolution as a person of wisdom.

Engagement: You may return to the beginning of the decision process multiple times to determine deeper and deeper levels of meaning. You will find that your means of responding to the situation will change. This is normal for large, significant events and you should have compassion for your need to revisit it over and over again.

Execution: As you execute in response to this important crisis you may be clear one moment and wallowing in despair the next. This is normal. Each time you experience a sense of confusion or end up feeling overwhelmed or depressed, do not give in to these feelings. Instead, return to the beginning of the process and work it again as if it contains new and important understandings regarding the old problem.

Outcomes:

What Should Happen: Crisis, real crisis, creates ongoing platforms for our work as human beings. Each time you reflect on this situation, you should learn new things about its impact and continuing value as a life directing force. It is like a large onion that keeps revealing deeper and deeper layers of wisdom.

What Can Go Wrong: The worst thing that can happen is if you allow the event to overwhelm you and your sense of self. If you lose your objectivity and sense of a larger order to things, you may allow your feelings and fears to consume you.

How to Fix It: When you lose your direction and feel as though you are losing control, return to the fundamentals of Grace. Many people find it not only comforting, but sustaining, to be reminded of the larger purpose to things. If you can see a larger purpose or outcome in an event, it may give you the sense of calm you need to continue on. Become flexible and curious and let go of your negative judgment. For example, in the aftermath of Florida's hurricane Andrew, many of its victims spoke of an important and sustaining sense of community and heroism. During the time of the crisis, both the best and the worst responses arose from its affected population. You will find similar comments after every major disaster.

If you are struggling in the situation and cannot find your way to the top, create a vision for how a person of Grace would handle the same situation. See if you can follow their lead. This may be a real person you know, or a fictitious person you create.

Advanced Intelligence:

These large-scale attacks on our sense of peace and control are very often life correcting events that cause us to step toward a destiny that was not part of our plan. The more you fight the event, the more you are fighting your own destiny.

Significant crisis showcase the need to combine all three fundamentals of Grace. To gracefully maneuver through life-changing events we need a sense of personal confidence, clarity regarding the meaning of the crisis and trust in a force larger than our own. If we focus on the three fundamental components of Grace as we navigate, they will become a part of us. That is the reward. It is a little like the saying, "The reward for patience is patience." The reward for trusting is Trust. The reward for being clear is Clarity, and the reward for finding a sense of self in a crisis is Confidence.

Issues	Possible Causes	Possible Pathways to Grace
Health crisis.	Blocked energy to a specific part of your body.	Identify a reason you may have emotionally blocked your energy to that location and work backwards to remove the block.
"Accident"	A wake up call regarding some aspect of your approach to life. Look for patterns of behavior or symbolic connections to the type of accident.	Absorb the message; change your life accordingly.

Issues	Possible Causes	Possible Pathways to Grace
Natural disaster	• You are at the site of this disaster in order to change your values or priorities. • Look for the life correcting nature of this event.	Determine what you have lost as a result of this disaster, and ask what that loss means to your journey. Many people who lose a loved one find a life of crusade as a result of that loss. What was missing that you must now find? How has this set you on a different path than the one you would have chosen?

Application #11

Actions in Sync with Your Sense of Self

Too often we view ourselves one way and circumstances cause us to act in another. How many of us, when faced with just the right set of fears, will do the unthinkable? Assume that being careless, insensitive or less than honest is below the standards we've set for ourselves, and yet we do it. Why? Grace is the ability to fight the odds, the influences and the fears and come out doing the right things even as we battle within.

Objective:

- To become a reflection of your values in all situations.
- To be comfortable stating who you are and what you stand for, even when stating the truth will set off a chain of events forcing you to give up something significant.

Prepare:

Define Your Initiative: All of us rationalize doing things for which we would judge others harshly. Whether or not we acknowledge it, our values are rarely black and white. We want to believe that our values are clearly defined, but in reality, most of us operate on a continuum. At one end of the continuum lies the optimal, if idealistic, response of *always* living each of our values consistently. On the other end lies the sub-optimal condition of living our values inconsistently. They are many issues and situations between these two extremes. Our challenge is to move toward *always*, no matter how deep the provocation to do otherwise.

Rarely   *Mostly live my values*   *Always live my values*
|_____|_____|

143

To work with this application you must be brutally honest. You must look at the current circumstances of your life and identify one specific situation where you are not being totally honest or you are not acting with a high level of integrity. You may need to ask the opinion of others in order to identify the situation accurately. Someone who knows you well, if asked the right question, will always give you the answer, often without having to think about it.

If you are struggling to identify a situation where you are not living with total authenticity, ask someone who knows you well the following question: "Is there any situation that you know of where you think I am not being totally honest with myself ?" Attempt to work with this situation even if you don't believe their answer.

Write a brief description of what you will work on in your journal!

The Challenge: You have gained something by not behaving totally in sync with your values. You will lose whatever that is. In order to move on, you must be prepared to let go of any safety net you are hanging onto.

To more fully live your values and your life, you may have to give up things that are comforting to you. You may have to turn down something rewarding, let go of a person who only partially meets your needs, or walk away from something that makes you feel safe.

The Skill Set: Be able to identify the thought processes behind your conclusions as a means to help others understand. For example, you may have to tell someone that you were initially afraid to tell them the truth because you were afraid that they would: 1) not handle it well, 2) judge you and your fears harshly, 3) fight you so hard that it would not be worth the effort, etc. You must communicate your newly understood feelings in a way that is not perceived as muddled or fearful, but instead as an objective assessment of your own weaknesses. This is a very powerful technique that allows others the room to be imperfect but still open to taking the risk required to accompany you in your authentic approach to a crisis.

Approach:

If you have been given something to work on by someone who knows you well, and you do not see what they see, be objective. If you feel defensive and are tempted to justify your choices or behaviors, take this as a clue that you are working on *exactly the right problem*. Become curious. Try to see what other person sees. Ask questions if you still think he or she is mistaken. Do not defend. Ask. Your approach to this problem must be totally open.

Examine the five-step process:

Critical Moment. Be very clear regarding the situation or behavior in which you or others perceive you to be out of sync with your values. If you are attempting to justify what you are doing, thinking, etc., assume the fear you want to identify is hidden within that justification.

Vision: Create a vision in which you see yourself move through any fear and find your way to a greater state of Clarity, Confidence and Trust. In the desired outcome there are no discrepancies between your behaviors and your ideals. For example, you might envision being able to live your values, even in a situation where it is particularly difficult to remain true to yourself. As a result, you come to know yourself better.

Assessment: The assessment step will be the most difficult of the five-steps in this application. You may be blind to your behaviors, and therefore, your motives. You may need to seek input and ask people why they think you are choosing to act as you are. Be careful not to seek justification for your choices; this will not move you along. You must determine if your fear of others' reactions is worth sabotaging your authenticity.

Engagement: In this application, engagement may entail going against your instincts in order to do the right thing. Once you understand *why* you are doing what you are doing, you can decide to live your truth regardless of the situation. Assume that the gap between you and your values is *not* the risks that you have identified, but the *skills* you need to live your values. You want to understand how to do so without manifesting the negative outcomes you fear. Decide to live your values so skillfully and with such Trust, Confidence and Clarity that the negative reactions you fear don't occur.

Execute: As you execute in sync with your values, it will probably create more critical moments to explore. Others may react negatively to the change. In rationalizing your own abdication from authentic behavior, you may have been protecting them. You may need to allow them to take responsibility for their own paths.

Outcomes:

What Should Happen: If you decide to adopt behavior that better reflects who you want to be, *and* you develop skills to go with your determination, you should find what was "unthinkable" before is now effortless. You should find that others are less reactive than you feared. You should find that you are now on a better path for everyone involved and as a result of your consistent behavior, your life is much less complicated. You have saved yourself future pain by dealing with the current situation more authentically and by eliminating the complicated maneuvers required to protect whatever you were protecting.

What Can Go Wrong: You may change your behavior in a way that ignores or does not account for the fact that others have been participating in your deceits. As a result, they may rebel or react with such force against your desire to be realistic and honest that you respond by crawling back into your shell and feeling victimized by the circumstance.

How to Fix It: Before you launch your new found enthusiasm for being honest, slow down and identify the fears that others may have. Their fears may also have kept you from reacting sooner. Find a way (see The Skills Set below) to communicate with others respectfully and yet firmly. You can help them understand why you'll no longer support situations that do not feel true to you. It is up to them to decide how to respond to your choices.

Advanced Intelligence:

By avoiding issues in the past you have helped to cause ongoing confusion. When you begin to address issues directly, you will gain the advantage of dealing with reality in a much more effective way. Often you will be helping others as well as yourself. You have all cooperated in dysfunctional behavior.

Issue	Possible Cause	Possible Path to Grace
Trying too hard to impress someone with your intelligence and having it backfire.	Insecurity in your own value and contribution.	Admit exactly what is going on with you at the time. Admit that your approach backfired and seemed disrespectful (this usually causes the other person to think it takes guts to admit your insecurities.) You cannot do this with needy expectations if you are to succeed. It is a clearing of the air, not another bid for attention.
Being dishonest with others due to pressure from someone in power.	Inability to see options, feeling a need to show deference for security reasons, etc.	Identify what you believe should be done and why. In a non-judgmental way, communicate to the person in power by identifying concerns. Offer alternatives that meet that person's needs as well as your own. See if there is a middle ground.
Allowing someone their misconceptions about how you feel because it is easier than popping his or her bubble.	• Laziness. • Inability to "hurt" others.	You will very likely have to burst the bubble sooner or later. Communicate your true feelings to them and allow them to make their own choices. If they refuse to hear you, then you should still act definitively no matter what you gain by allowing the status quo.

Application # 12

Level II

Knowing Your Purpose

Do you know your essence? If you were asked to define the core of who you are in one word, how quickly would you be able to respond? This is not an easy question. There are very few individuals who are clear about the "indispensable or intrinsic properties that characterize or identify" who they are. We are confused by our training and the demands we place upon ourselves, both of which cause us to think in terms of who we're *supposed* to be instead of who we *are*. If you cannot quickly identify who you are, at the most intimate level (in one word) you have work to do.

Objective:

- To develop an understanding of self. This understanding becomes the anchor in confusing and challenging circumstances.
- To know yourself so well, and to be so in love with who you are, that you cannot imagine subverting it for anyone or any thing.

Prepare:

Define Your Initiative: Identify a circumstance or situation in which you are confused and possibly unstable due to your confusion. You may not be sure why you are in the situation or what you are supposed to do. You may feel a pull in multiple directions simultaneously. You may be receiving mixed messages about what is expected of you.

Write a brief description of what you will work on in your journal!

The Challenge: Remembering that you are exactly where you are supposed to be may be your biggest challenge. When things are not working effortlessly, it is easy to think that you are in the wrong place at the wrong time. Stay curious about why you are supposed to be in this situation.

The Skill Set: First, you must be able to identify who you are with true clarity. Find a way to contribute your essence to the circumstance. You might expand that capacity to include helping others identify and apply *their* true essence.

Remember that events do not unfold just because you want them to. This is a lesson in ego management. Recognizing that you are connected and dependent on others is also important. This application is *Level II* primarily because it is so integrated with the core value of others with whom you interact.

Approach:

In order to find resolution, you may need to recall a situation in which you were truly in the flow. Situations where you were operating at peak often tell you a lot about your essence. Identify an intrinsic value you brought to the situation.

When you understand the value you have added at key moments in the past, it is often easier to determine what you have to contribute during confusing times. Exploring your past is a way of gaining confidence about why you, why now, why here.

Examine the five-step process:

Critical Moment: Identify what you are feeling about the situation you are exploring and why you feel that way. Since the process being suggested requires exploring two situations at the same time, also identify what you were feeling and why about the peak performance scenario. You are going to compare and contrast the two circumstances.

Vision: Take a slightly different approach to the visioning step. This time, identify what it was about *you,* specifically and uniquely, that allowed you to be so effective in the peak situation. See if you can find one word to describe who you were and what your greatest contribution was at the time.

Place the word which describes you here:

_____

Examine the word carefully. Does it truly describe *you* or does it describe who you were at that time?

When identifying the words that describe your essence, you will usually choose words that apply to a specific value that is intrinsic to your being. For example, words like: warrior, teacher, crusader, truth-teller, direct, nurturer, etc. Do not question your instincts. Instead, question why you might be withholding your essence in the difficult situation you are currently addressing.

Refine your vision for the current situation to include the opportunity to apply the core essence of who you are. Assume that the situation needs you to contribute your intrinsic value.

Assessment: Identify what has held you back from asserting your unique contribution. What are you afraid of? What are the risks of doing so? What might be the risks of not asserting your core characteristic into this situation?

Engagement: Decide what you will do next by identifying a way to apply your essence to the situation. If this is a joint effort, you may want to ask others if they can identify their own intrinsic value and apply it to solving the problem at hand as well.

Execution: Remain very conscious as you apply the agreed upon solution to this problem. Ask yourself who you are (one word) and how to use that essence in this moment most effectively. Be very clear about what holds you back and how to reassert yourself in a way that is confident, clear, and trusting.

Outcomes:

What Should Happen: When you are able to find your own value you, exhibit confidence which is compelling to others. You may have been trying to have all the answers as opposed to having an approach. If you expected yourself to have all the answers even when you were unsure, you may have caused others to doubt you and possibly resist. When you relinquish your need to know the answers, and instead, approach the problem by applying your essence, others become more trusting, more cooperative and ultimately clearer about their own, unique contribution.

What Can Go Wrong: You may decide that your essence is not producing the desired outcome in the current environment or situation. You may want to determine if the problem is due to a lack of skill. For example, suppose you know your core essence to be one of truth and directness. Perhaps you are being truthful or direct in a way that feels abusive to another's sense of *his or her* value. You may simply need to learn finesse.

How to Fix It: If you fear that who you are is not valued, you are making a mistake. Assume instead that you are applying 'who you are' in a way that may be diminishing to others. Identify the skill set you may be missing and work on it. Then, re-approach the issue, again with your essence, and see if you realize a better outcome. For example, the person you once assumed did not want to hear the truth may not have wanted to hear the truth in a way that threatened his or her ego or sense of self. When you find more skillful ways to deliver your truth, you may find that previous resistance melts away.

Advanced Intelligence:

Finding and knowing your core can take years of introspection. Over time, you will discover deeper and deeper levels of truth regarding your sense of self, your purpose and your contribution. Each discovery validates the previous discovery and adds a dimension or sense of richness to your self assessment.

Issue	Possible Cause/Belief	Possible Path to Grace
You feel unsupported in capitalizing on your strengths.	You have learned something about yourself that is incorrect. You may think that willing something to happen is your core and now others are not responding.	Go deeper. For example, if you are good at forcing things to happen and it isn't working this time, see if there is a different reason that it has worked for you in the past.
The environment is asking you to do something that is against everything you believe about yourself.	This may be a challenge from the Universe to see if you have both the strength and conviction to exhibit your values in a situation where it is unpopular.	Find a way to express your beliefs which is accepting of the other people involved. Bring rather than force them along a path to a higher plane. Assume a leadership cloak rather than being judgmental.
You believe that to exhibit your core in this environment would be highly self-destructive.	You share responsibility for creating this environment. Even as you judge others, you must acknowledge that your own fear has caused you to play along. Environments are a reflection of each participant's will.	• If you want to find Grace, you will have to find a way to be authentic in a situation even when it pushes you into a mold you do not like. What is it worth to you? • Be clear about your essence. Attempt to use it in this situation to break the ice and create change.

TRUST

Application # 13

Level I

Rewriting History

Crises are a part of life. Mastering Grace means that you have the ability to stay balanced and react with calm to crisis, no matter how difficult. Many of us are like Charlie Brown when, every time something goes wrong, he puts his hands over his ears and says, "We're doomed!" If you are someone who anticipates crisis in every thing that does not fit into your "plan", you will find that your path to Grace is difficult. Hopefully, if you have worked through the previous applications diligently, you are ready to let go of some of the fear that pervades your existence. You should find the following application life changing.

Objective:

1. To accept crisis as a means to redirect your path in a positive way.
2. To learn to trust in a greater purpose, particularly during events that may cause you to doubt that greater purpose the most.

Prepare:

Define Your Initiative: Find a moment in your past that represents a significant crisis for you. You want to choose one of those moments where life was forever different as a result of the crisis. This application is intended to help you find a new view of an old event.

Write a brief description of what you will work on in your journal!

The Challenge: The most difficult aspect to finding new wisdom in an old event is that thoughts are often habits. You will need to erase your thoughts about this past event in order to find new ones.
The Skill Set: Visualization is a very helpful skill. To find the impact on your current thinking of an event that is finished, you will use visualization.

Create a new visualization of your past by changing or eliminating a critical moment in your life and then allowing your brain to create a picture of how your life might have unfolded if it had never occurred. Pick up the strings of your life at the moment of the old crisis, and project your life outward as if the event had never occurred. Identify who you might have become without the crisis, and determine if that person is as fully formed as the one who came through the crisis.

Approach:

Assume that crisis from your past continues to impact how you view both the present and the future. Without the processing being suggested in this application, it is highly likely that the past crisis have cast a residual negative mantle over your experiences. You will want to approach this exercise with curiosity and openness to receive the maximum benefit.

Examine the five-step process:

Critical Moment: Study the effect of the crisis carefully. Identify what you believe to be its impact on your life in terms of both feelings and fears. Examine your beliefs about this crisis' negative impact on you and your life. Are you fearful in some situations as a result? Do you hold back from fully committing yourself? Are you in some way diminished in your own eyes because of it? Be ruthlessly honest as you explore the nature of this crisis' impact on current and future critical moments in your life.

Vision: Your vision is to complete this application with a greater understanding of the gift in the crisis. After doing this application on an old crisis, you want to see its power in defining who you are and how you travel your life's path. Your stated vision might be: I will come to a new and greater understanding of this crisis' benefit to me and in doing so, will let go of its negative impact and move past any fear or anger I am still holding.

Assessment: This is the most meaningful step in this particular application. Look at your life starting from the moment the crisis occurred. Ask yourself the following questions and allow yourself time to explore and answer each question both intuitively and logically:

If I were to turn time back to shortly before the crisis occurred and project my life forward from that point as if the crisis had never happened, what would be different about my life?

Who would I be?

How would I respond differently than I respond now?

What did I learn from the crisis?

If I compare myself to who I would have been without the crisis, in what way am I internally different? What have I lost? What have I gained?

Engagement: As you engage with *current* challenging situations, reflect on your reactions. What would you do differently if you had never been through the crisis from your past that you are now exploring? How is this current situation related? Does this new situation represent a symbol of how far you have come or does it represent a way in which you have let the other crisis handicap and cripple you?

The very nature of a current problem may represent either an area of growth or of atrophy which is affected by your processing of the original crisis.

Execution: Examine current events in your life and determine how to use your evaluation of the past crisis to improve how you respond now.

Outcomes:

What Should Happen: By imagining your life without the crisis, you will almost always find that you are in a very different place than you would have been if it had never happened. You may identify both pluses and minuses, but most people find a sense of completeness *within* themselves which would be absent without having experienced the past crisis in their lives.

159

Many find that they dislike or do not respect the person they *would have* become without the crisis. Most people recognize a respect for self which they have earned through processing a major event. Others sometimes struggle to describe personal changes that have occurred as a result of the crisis. However, when these people describe who they would be without the crisis, they often articulate a sense of being emptier and less relevant.

What Can Go Wrong: There are times when you may be so angry or afraid that you are unable to see the larger picture or purpose. Continue to study the concept of trust so that, in the big moments, you simply trust in the underlying purpose without needing to *know.* Obviously, this is an advanced skill. In some religions, they call it Faith.

How to Fix It: When you cannot find a purpose in a crisis, you may need to give it time. In the short-term, while you wait for clarity, it is appropriate to allow yourself to be angry. Sometimes, anger gives you the strength necessary to reach the next level of understanding. Be kind to yourself; accept your need to process things your own way. Be very careful not to let anger become the end result. Be watchful and ruthless in stopping a pattern of anger. It is self-destructive.

Advanced Intelligence:

Major crises can change the direction of our lives. If a crisis caused you to stretch farther, become more, or grow faster, then you have experienced a primary facet of trust. As you move toward more and more consistent Grace you begin to understand that the Universe *always* has a purpose for even the most insignificant disappointments in our lives. If we learn to stop and identify what that purpose might be, we save ourselves much anxiety and struggle.

Below are some examples of life-changing, seemingly negative events and some possible rewrites. If the rewrites do not feel good to you, write your own. The point is not to discount or diminish the impact of serious and sad events; it's to find the positive in them so that your process becomes a little easier.

Issues	Cause/Belief	Possible Path to Grace
Having a child with a life threatening illness.	Sense of unfairness in life.	Assume that this is a deliberate intervention in your life and your evolution as a human being. Perhaps you needed to learn how to accept imperfection. Perhaps this is causing you to live your life in a much more meaningful way than if everything had gone as planned. Possibly this matter is bringing people into your life you would never have met. Think as if this child is a soul who has agreed to this challenge for its own development as well as yours.

Having a life threatening illness.	You may think of yourself as a helpless victim.	Engage in the process of coping with this disease. Approach it as if it is teaching you things about you and what you want to learn.
Loss of a key relationship through death or choice (not necessarily your choice).	You may feel overwhelmed by a sense of emptiness, fear of the future, feelings of failure, sense of rejection or low self-esteem.	Ask yourself what purpose, in a positive sense, the emptiness may be serving. For example, is it creating an open space in which to do something? What might that be? If you have lost a key relationship with someone through choice (theirs or yours), become very clear about the purpose the relationship has served in your life and what is now opening up for you as a result of its loss.

Application #14

Level II

Riding the Wave

Hopefully, during the last application you were able to rewrite your history in a way that makes everything that has occurred seem somehow different to you. If you were successful in doing so, the demands of this application may seem more rational and doable. When we started the process of attempting to find Grace in difficult situations, you were warned that you probably have life patterns which are working against your success. Now we are going to work to create a sense of trust in the larger purpose behind your life so that you can more readily move into "Super-Positioning" when facing difficult challenges.

Objective:

- To move quickly into Super Positioning by identifying a larger purpose in the most mundane circumstance.
- To develop a habit of trusting that each and every moment is filled with Grace.
- To go looking for Grace when it is not readily apparent.

Prepare:

Define Your Initiative: Any problem will do, no matter how mundane. You are going to attempt to make Trust an automatic response. Any situation where you are frustrated or angry will work.

Write a brief description of what you will work on in your journal!

The Challenge: Are you able to stop in the moment and identify a greater purpose for this obstacle? This is a Level II application because it requires you to use the concept of Grace moment to moment; whenever something disturbs you. People who master this never hesitate. They miss their plane and they look for who they are supposed to meet on the next flight. They

163

stub their toe and they wonder why they are supposed to slow down. Their car breaks down and they look for the adventure they are supposed to have.

The Skill Set: You will assume that there is a Force that is control and that all events are meaningful. Nothing happens by accident. The skill comes in your ability to identify the law of cause and effect in every situation. So, for example, a person wounds you in some way and you start by assuming that this is a gift from the Universe. There are two things to look for. The first is whether or not you have wounded someone else in a similar fashion or might have been intending to do so. The second is to assume that the person who wounded you will have to learn this lesson in the future. Revenge is pointless and only keeps you in the loop. Another application of this understanding is to look for how this situation may be redirecting your path.

Approach:

You have the opportunity to make any moment important. Recognize that each moment may be the critical moment that could change your life if you respond properly. By now, you know if you tend to be timid, controlling, angry, or passive-aggressive in response to challenges. Assume that behind any disruption or challenge to the easy flow of your life is a force operating for the greater good. As you move through this application, instead of your typical, patterned, knee-jerk response, describe the moment as a symptom of this same force directing you to a better place.

Examine the five-step process:

Critical Moment: With whatever problem you are confronting, ask yourself how you *want* to respond. Write it down. Do you want to scream, attack, or hide? Why? What do those responses tell you about yourself?

Vision: Instead of doing what you want to do, create a vision of yourself handling this situation effortlessly and with minimal emotion. If anything, assume that you will handle this moment with humor.

Assessment: This is your key step to success in handling any moment with Grace. Take the situation that you have chosen and assume that it has been created for your benefit. If this situation is for your benefit, then your job is to identify the reason why. Your reason does not have to be true in order for it to help you process this moment with Grace. Your rationale should make some logical sense, and if possible, it should make you smile! For example, the traffic jam is to allow you to listen to music and arrive at your destination more relaxed. If you get angry or tense, you miss the point. You will still be late, but you will also arrive in a less productive state.

Engagement: After you determine a possible reason the Universe arranged this situation for your benefit; behave as though the reason you invented is true. Do not attempt to change the situation or control it. Find a way to flow with it. Have the Grace to change the things you can and take advantage of the things you cannot, as if they were a wonderful present in a funny package.

Execution: When you trust that this moment was given to you as a gift, you should find that your interactions with others improve dramatically. You gain an ability to be patient and not push, your need to punish people who attempt to hurt you goes away, and your whole attitude toward adversity becomes "Zen-like". Execution becomes effortless and flowing, as it should be.

Outcomes:

What Should Happen: If you stop in the moment and attribute a positive reason to a normally frustrating circumstance, your responses will become more focused and purposeful. What had previously appeared to be a problem should now become a sign meant to keep you from making a mistake, moving too soon, etc. Over time you will increase your sense of the "rightness" of how things work. You will be less reactive as your beliefs change to include a great trust in the benevolent Force on your side.

What Can Go Wrong: You may have a tendency to recognize what you have lost rather than what you have gained. If the situation involves another person and the other person appears to be successful in their efforts to diminish your outcome, you may retain some anger or bitterness. It may appear to you that the other person has won and you have lost.

How to Fix It: Stay "real" with what is happening. While others may look successful, you must identify whether it is really true. Do people like her? Do they respect him? Is he really any good at what he does or will he fail at some point in the future when he is highly visible? You may have to stand back and watch for a while to see the truth, but never doubt it. He will "get his". And you will "get yours" - just be aware of what you are earning for yourself and choose carefully.

Advanced Intelligence: As you begin to notice how often events work in your favor if you get out of the way, you may also observe that they work for others in the same way. Suppose you play the bull-fighter and step out of the way of a person attempting to undermine you. He or she will undoubtedly cause trouble for himself (or herself) if you stay out of the way. The "trouble" is a gift designed to help the person understand that the gains of undermining someone are temporary or less than satisfying. If, instead, you follow old patterns and fight with the person to protect your turf, it is likely that you'll both be learning this lesson.

Issue	Cause /belief	Path to Grace
Your primary relationship just broke off against your will. You are devastated.	You believe that you might not replace the relationship and that you will be alone.	You were already alone because you were with a person who did not want to be with you. Now you have hope.

Issue	Cause /belief	Path to Grace
You have a boss who wants to take credit for what you did.	You believe that your career will lose momentum if this person succeeds and you want to fight it.	Assume that you are being given time to really develop your foundation before your next promotion. Assume this is the Universe's plan and that the current situation is a means to slow you down. The progression of your career has nothing to do with what your boss chooses to do. Assume that their lesson will come to them without you pointing the finger.
Your house is destroyed in a hurricane and you lose everything.	You fear that you will never catch up with where you were; that you may never get over the sense of devastation.	First, you lived. Second, you have a wonderful opportunity to rethink your life. You are free to decide where you want to live and what is really important. Others may live a shallow life, but you have not been allowed to. Think about having a blank slate to start over and use it wisely!

Application #15

Level I

Building Your Plan into Theirs

In any endeavor, Ego is often the biggest distraction. The need to assert oneself, one's ideas, and one's power will often cause a fall from Grace. You may win the immediate battle, but the disruption you have created could be your own downfall. The next two applications are essential in their relevance to your journey toward Grace. The first application (Application #15-Level I) will evolve your skill in adapting your ideas and agendas into the ideas and agendas of others. The second (Application #16-Level II) will develop your ability to control your attitude regarding individuals who pose the most difficulty for you.

Objective:

- To be able to identify why another person's idea is an enhancement of your own thoughts and intentions.
- To put your ego aside and make the outcome more important than you.

Prepare:

Define Your Initiative: Identify any issue where you are at odds with one or more people. This might be in terms of a solution, an approach or next steps on some initiative.

Write a brief description of what you will work on in your journal!

The Challenge: The biggest challenge in this application is letting go of your own biases enough to find the hidden treasures in opposition. You may have a strong reaction to what appears to be nonsense in the other person's point of view. Be careful that you do not miss the opportunity represented by his or her position.

The Skill Set: If you are put-off by seemingly illogical suggestions or solutions, do not show your reaction. Instead, see if you can identify the fear represented by the other person's or peoples' ideas. Sometimes their idea is a means to protect them from something they fear. It is probably not your fear or the idea would not seem so far out to you. Once you think you have identified the fear behind their suggestion, see if you can also identify the relevance of that fear on a larger scale. Who else might share their fear and potentially impact the result? If you address the fear in your solution, you might save yourself problems later.

Approach:

This exercise will challenge your ability to set aside emotions, biases, and any sense of fear regarding an outcome or problem resolution that is not designed solely by you. Even if another person's ideas do not resonate with your own, you must find the value in their approach and integrate it into your approach.

Examine the five-step process:

Critical Moment: As you examine the issue and the fact that you are at odds with someone over its resolution, assume that you may be missing something that the other person sees. Identify clearly what it is that you dislike or fear about the other person's approach.

Vision: Envision a solution which incorporates the other person's view into your own or vice versa. Think of a perfect resolution to the issue which includes everyone feeling a part of and contributing to the result.

Assessment: Assume that the other person's considerations include an understanding of a fear you do not have. The person who is at odds with you over the resolution of this issue may represent a small percentage of your solution that you would not have seen without their opposition. Your job is to identify the risks that you might have missed without the distraction. Acknowledge how your vision has been enhanced by others who see the problem differently.

Engagement: As you reflect on the direction you will take, identify how you will include the solutions presented by others. If another person outranks you or out-positions you with his or her solution, be creative about including your design *into* their solution as opposed to the other way around.

Execution: Be sure to keep in mind what you have learned about your audience through the assessment process. Remember that this information was not apparent to you at first because it did not represent your personal fears or issues. Stay alert as you execute for evidence of the other's concerns. You can respond should they surface.

Outcomes:

What Should Happen: If you are respectful of others' points of view, and you integrate those points of view into your thinking and your solutions, you should see everyone beginning to cooperate in new ways. You should also see that the effectiveness of your solution is enhanced by your willingness to set aside judgment. You do not have to win; you do not have to be right. You allow for the fact that others may see and know things that are invisible to you. You should feel an amazing sense of release. By working more collaboratively, you will take a lot of pressure off yourself.

What Can Go Wrong: Your logic may get in your way. For example, you may know that the other person is being illogical and you refuse to agree with their proposed direction because it feels so illogical. What you forget is that their 'illogical' response represents something deeper and hidden to you. Whatever the other person is reacting to could affect your solution's ultimate effectiveness.

How to Fix It: Even when the other person seems disconnected from reality, assume that there is important data hidden within their reaction. Find the data. Be curious. Assume you have missed something. You will realize that no matter how ill-conceived someone else's idea might seem it will always contain an element that you need. You will begin to have more respect for points of view that previously may have seemed weak or fearful. If you apply this concept to your decision-making, you may find it tempers your arrogance.

Advanced Intelligence: Sometimes the organization, family, or entity affected by your solution is not advanced enough to utilize your solution. You may have to temper your ideal to fit the reality of the circumstance. Rather than make others feel inadequate or foolish, a person of Grace allows others to catch up in their own time. He or she is patient with partial acceptance of his or her ideas.

Potential problems and solutions below:

Issue	Cause/Belief	Path to Grace
Others diffuse the quality of what you have created.	You believe that they do not want to implement something that they did not invent.	• Assume the real fear is that they do not understand or they are not sure how to implement your solution. They may not want to say that to you for fear of appearing stupid. • Your choice is to accept their state of readiness, or attempt to bring them gently along to where you are.
A person in positional power is choosing the safe response to a crisis and you know that they are ultimately missing the opportunity to deal with it effectively.	You may be underestimating the danger to others in what you suggest. You may be putting others at risk by focusing on the most logical resolution to an issue or problem.	Identify what they are afraid of and take it seriously. Build a solution to that risk into your plan, or adjust your plan.

Issue	Cause/Belief	Path to Grace
Someone has a need to always be right. He or she cannot hear or appreciate anyone else's ideas.	You are making them feel inadequate and their response is to be 'right' at all costs.	Take responsibility for the fact that you are intimidating the other person. Rather than discount their response as irrelevant or weak, build it into how you approach the solution. Make it about them and watch how they let go.

Application # 16

Level II

Becoming One with Your Adversaries

Think about the person for whom you have nothing but contempt. Imagine being understanding and even compassionate toward that person. Perhaps it is rather obvious why this is a *Level II* application.

Objective:

- To understand what motivates your opponents.
- To understand and empathize with their point of view.
- To eliminate all judgmental feelings toward your adversary.
- To experience yourself from your enemy's point of view in such a way that your attitudes and behaviors automatically change.

Prepare:

Define Your Initiative: Choose your poison. Whom do you want to work on? Pick an issue which exists between you and this person and resolve to work it through to a Graceful conclusion (effortless flow).

Write a brief description of what you will work on in your journal!

The Challenge: It is always difficult to let go of your feelings in this kind of situation. Whenever you have an intense reaction to someone, that person represents a hidden fear. It is probable that this person reminds you of something or someone from your past. The very thought of no longer holding this person in contempt may feel like giving up a part of who you are.

Your contempt protects you. Unfortunately, instead of protecting you it makes you a target. Finding Grace is the only real protection. Your sense of confidence and clarity about who this person is will be your protection.

Trusting that the Universe put this person in your path to help you is your salvation.

The Skill Set: Putting yourself into another person's experience is an advanced skill. Visualization is once again a helpful tool. Using the situation you've chosen, imagine yourself as if you were the *other* person.

Approach:

Your job, as you work through this particular problem with this person is to experience the issue from his or her side. This means that you not only have to try to understand the other point of view, but you must try to experience what it is like to be them. In particular, you must experience what it is like to be them as they attempt to relate to you.

Examine the five-step process:

Critical Moment: This person's presence in your life represents a critical opportunity to change something inside of you. If this person had no impact on you, there would be nothing to learn. Identify what you feel in this person's presence and why you think you feel that way.

Vision: Try to create a vision where you imagine yourself feeling in sync with this person. In your vision, you are in sync and comfortable and have a benevolent and easy feeling around them. You don't have to love them, but you do want to be at ease. You are no longer angry or fearful of this person and they no longer cause you a strong emotion of any kind.

Assessment: Identify all of the risks you feel this person represents for you. Then, imagine that you represent similar risks to them. While this is particularly hard to imagine if the person appears to hold all of the positional power in the situation, be assured that if you are feeling intense feelings regarding them, it's mutual.

Assume that you threaten or anger the other person with intensity similar to what you feel. Make a list of ways that you might threaten them. This exercise should be enlightening. Use this knowledge to understand their point of view.

You may come to the conclusion that it is that impossible for you to ever work well with this person and it is time to "fold 'em". However, when you make a decision to fold 'em it should be done from a place of clarity, not angst. You are probably not finished until this person holds no more threat for you.

Try to identify with the other person's concerns or fears. You do not have to agree. You are simply trying to imagine what it is like for them to push forward with your agenda in your way.

Engagement: Be creative. Look for a new solution. This new solution must fit your criteria for success and also be less threatening for your enemy. At this point you are just being creative. You have made no commitment. Be curious. Ask questions. See if you can find common ground. Do not allow yourself to become frustrated as you seek a way to work with this person. Try something new.

Execution: Test yourself by discussing with the person different ways to look at the outcome. See if the interaction is easier now that you've tried to build a solution with their point of view in mind.

Outcomes:

What Should Happen: When you are clear about your enemy's fears and do your best to not trigger them, your path to the outcome should be easier and less contentious. By being respectful of the impact you have on this person and consciously managing that impact, some of the tension between the two of you should ease.

What Can Go Wrong: You may be too analytical in your approach to this issue. You may figure everything out but fail to change. You may manipulate the pieces differently and yet, get the same result. To get a meaningful result from this application you must examine the situation through your feelings. Just figuring out your opponent is unlikely to be enough.

How to Fix It: Go back and reassess. This time, *be* the other person and *experience* you as if you are looking through the other person's eyes. Feel what he or she feels when facing you across the room or table. Ask yourself if this is what you want others to feel when they are around you. Decide if you want to be the kind of person who intimidates others, angers others or annoys others. Decide if you want to be a person of Grace, or the person you are now in this relationship.

Advanced Intelligence:

To get to a place of ease with your enemy, you may have to pretend to be that person and understand how it feels for him or her to interact with you. You may find that you have rationalized and justified abusive and disrespectful behavior. When you experience *you* from the other person's perspective, it is possible that you will be flabbergasted at how awful you have been. This would be the most positive outcome. If you experience the other person's feelings, and you are dismayed, you will never treat that person as poorly again.

Some issues and resolutions below:

Issue	Cause/Belief	Path to Grace
Your boss is a fool who has loyalties to subordinates who are incompetent. He is angry with you for pointing out their incompetence. You feel he should be grateful.	You believe that you are a crusader for what is right and should be rewarded for caring so much.	Imagine how it feels to be your boss when you walk into a room. See how difficult you are and how difficult you make his life by asking him to treat your peers as if they are as incompetent as you think they are. Allow yourself to feel how hard you are to be around and how hard it would be to deal with someone who is that strident and angry all the time.
Your peer is incompetent but somehow never held accountable. He screams at you in meetings and bullies your subordinates.	You are aghast that he is allowed to behave in that way and you cannot stand to be in the same room with him.	You get inside of him and his feelings and realize how afraid he is. You imagine what it feels like to interact with you and you realize he feels your contempt for him and he is reacting against that contempt. You feel what it would be like to have someone look at you with similar contempt.

Application #17

<u>Gaining Commitment</u>

You do not live in a vacuum. The ability to achieve what you want in your life is always impacted by the behaviors and actions of others. To be effective, you cannot just force your way to the end result. You must learn to work with the idiosyncrasies of individuals who have somehow aligned themselves to be a part of your journey. Do you know what they want? Do you care?

Objective:

- To gain more support for your agenda by tapping into the essence and contributions of others.
- To connect all activity to a larger purpose and share that connection in a way that helps others to adjust their thinking.
- To learn to avoid initiating activities through fear.

Prepare:

Define Your Initiative: Identify a situation in which you need the support of others to be effective. This can be either a personal or a professional objective. You may want to read through the steps below before you choose.

<u>Write a brief description of what you will work on in your journal!</u>

The Challenge: The biggest challenge is likely to be the need to slow down and take the time to understand others before making a decision. Over time, as you trust yourself more, it becomes even more tempting to hurry the process without doing your homework.

The Skill Set: You must continue to improve your ability to sort through the facts to determine the deeper purpose for both actions and people.

Hopefully, you have successfully applied these skills to yourself. Now you are spreading your net and attempting to include others in the process.

Approach:

There are at least two layers you must explore. The first layer is your own level of commitment to the end result. Identify if you are truly passionate about the outcome. If you are approaching it in a confused or unfocused way, you will find that others are unlikely to follow your lead.

The second layer of understanding explores the response of those upon whom you must depend for success. What if they are not taking responsibility for their part? This application explores the absence of true commitment at a deeper level than we have in previous applications. Identify whether you and those you depend on express a sense of purpose in being part of the activity. If the activity seems meaningless, you and others will treat it as if it is meaningless.

Examine the five-step process:

Critical Moment: Assume that this project or initiative is a test for how connected you are to your own destiny. How does this initiative apply to your essence and what you are doing with your life? Can you see a purpose to this activity which enables your journey? You must look deeper than, "this is my job" or this definition of the critical moment will have no meaning. Are you learning things that you need to learn in order to fulfill your purpose? Are you doing something that has meaning for the organization with which you are affiliated (family, corporation, country, etc)?

As you examine the lives of the other participants, can you connect to them in a way that offers clarity about who they are and how this initiative affects their growth, purpose, etc? Can you make that connection at the deeper level of essence? Do you have a sense of the other participants' essence?

Vision: Envision that the initiative you've chosen will be a full expression of the creativity and essence of the individuals involved. How can you grow your and others' sense of self through your participation in this initiative?

182

The ability to connect to a larger purpose resides within any activity. You must be clever and diligent enough to look for it.

Assessment: Identify a one word description for each participant's essence as you did for yourself in Application # 12. You will find that it is easier to do for others, but make sure you test your assumptions. Determine how you will evolve this initiative to speak to a larger purpose. For example, suppose you have chosen "I want to move to California to take a new job" and your family is resisting. Are you clear about how this new job fits into your larger purpose (as opposed to being able to make more money and gain more positional power)?

Thoroughly examine the risks and rewards of your chosen initiative *as they relate to your destiny*. Then, assess and identify the essence of each participant and how the risks and rewards impact them. Don't be satisfied with whether or not they are popular with or easy on them. Too often decisions of this nature are dictated by the path of least resistance. Such a path does not entitle anyone to Grace. You may need to engage with the other participants to discuss their opinion after you have formed some preliminary conclusions.

Engagement: In this step, you decide how to proceed, both independently and in collaboration with other participants. You will want to help everyone reach a higher plane with their approach. Some conversation around essence, purpose and contribution is worthwhile.

Execution: After the decisions have been made, you may find that others become faint of heart in the face of their commitments. You may, repeatedly, have to help them deal with their fears and their sense of purpose.

Outcomes:

What Should Happen: This is clearly an advanced application of Grace. It is also a preparation for one of the more advanced concepts in human interaction (Partnering) which you will encounter in the next application. To move through this initiative, you must understand others more deeply than you may have been inclined to do in the past. This may be unfamiliar territory, but your interactions with others will reach a new plane due to the energy you expend and the attention you apply. A new level of teamwork and understanding should emerge. Even if the outcome is not seamless or effortless, the learning you and others go through will change all subsequent interactions between you.

What Can Go Wrong: The other participants may not be ready to give up their view of what they want. They may resist looking deeper because it is to hard. They may resist taking responsibility for their own destiny because they want someone else to do it for them. They will fight you and fight your belief that each event, initiative or circumstance has meaning.

How to Fix It: You cannot fix others if they do not want to be fixed. However, you can still achieve your own effortless flow in spite of their response. How? By being clear and offering others choice. If you are clear that your choice aligns to your personal destiny and you believe others involved will gain more than they'll lose by agreeing to support your choice, then you will need to make some decisions. If the other participants are young, without a large life experience to draw from, you may need to trust your assessment that this experience will broaden their horizons, make the decision for them and accept that they may not appreciate your choice. You will need to let go of guilt and its ability to manipulate your feelings.

It is appropriate to make decisions affecting others when you are clear that they are responding out of fear rather than clarity, confidence and trust. When your response is coming from a place of confidence, clarity and trust, it is called leadership.

Advanced Intelligence:

A person of Grace is always conscious and respectful of the potential in others. He or she is aware of the reality of human uniqueness and that each person has a purpose and contribution. A person of Grace is always attempting to connect to the underlying force in themselves and others. Such a view of life creates a greater depth and vitality in the person and in those with whom he or she connects.

Possible issues and solutions:

Issue	Cause/ Belief	Path to Grace
You are working on something you believe to be important to the future of the organization (family, corporation, etc). Others are not on board.	They cannot see the same connection to the well being of the organization that you see. They are not seeing a connection to themselves.	Spend more time with them exploring their hopes and aspirations. Help them find the connection.
You have been forced to work on something in which you see no connection or purpose.	You believe it to be a meaningless activity.	Identify the possible connection to your own need for discipline, cooperation and responding to the needs of the person who created this activity. Try to help that person by accommodating them or by offering a solution which alleviates his or her fear or need.

Application #18

Level II

Partnering

Partnering is one of the most difficult realities to achieve when working with others. To partner effectively, you must have mutual respect, excellent communication, impeccable integrity, an ability to be flexible as outlined in previous applications and a willingness to look in the mirror when things break down. You must also have Clarity, Confidence and Trust in order to create true partnership. Or you must be willing to pull out of a partnership that is failing you.

According to Webster's Dictionary, a partnership implies a relationship, usually between two people, in which each person has equal status and independence, but also unspoken or formal obligation to the other or others.

Objective:

- To understand and participate effectively in the demands of a partnership, while remaining aware of the true nature of partnering.
- To know and understand when a partnership is failing and to act appropriately in such a circumstance to improve the flow of events in your life.

Prepare:

Define Your Initiative: Examine a current partnership that does not feel effortless to you. If no current situation fits this description, examine a past partnership for the learning that can still be cultivated.

Write a brief description of what you will work on in your journal!

The Challenge: Creating working partnerships is one of the riskier things any human can take on. By "working partnership", this text is referring to

187

working within the definition of an equal, yet independent relationship where both parties are in agreement regarding execution. Risk lies in each individual's understanding of what it takes to unravel a partnership that isn't working and how those understandings may differ. *Before* you enter into a partnership, be sure that you have what it takes to disengage if it does not work.

If you do not believe that you have what it takes to disengage, you may be too needy to even consider such a venture. A legally bound arrangement is not necessarily a guarantee. If you are depending on the formal, binding nature of a partnership to protect you, you probably do not have the clarity or the confidence to be successful.

There is a big difference between being committed to making it work and thinking that the legality or formal nature of a partnership will make it work. If you are hoping that a formality will cause the other person to be who you want them to be, you are being naive and foolish.

The Skill Set: The skill set needed to help a partnership reach its potential is extensive. You must have the communication skills to interact honestly and the finesse to work around big egos. You may need to build sophistication in just about every application in this text to have a partnership that feeds your life as well as your soul. Finally, you must know when to 'hold em' and when to 'fold em' if you are committed to living a life of Grace.

Due to human nature and the nature of partnerships, you must constantly reevaluate whether your partnerships are working and be prepared to make hard decisions if they are not. There is nothing more vitalizing than a working partnership and nothing more vitality-robbing than a poor one. If you believe that your commitment means you must stay with the partnership even if the other person is not prepared to meet their commitments or obligations, then you have sold your soul for the comfort of a legal agreement.

Approach:

How to approach this problem: Because of the legal and emotional connections of partnerships, this is one of the more difficult circumstances in which to remain clear, unbiased, and confident. Become as uncluttered as possible regarding the relationship's true nature. Decide whether it can be defined as a partnership. Be clear about your own fears related to addressing problems within the partnership. Set aside those fears until after you have clarity.

Examine the five-step process:

Critical Moment: Ask yourself what you are feeling about this partnership, and why. Examine your relationship to this partner in terms of your essence. Does this partner value your essence and do they exhibit that value in their interactions with you?

Vision: In any partnership, you must have a clear vision of how you need and want it to work. Take the time to create a clear vision of how this partnership must work in order for you to feel satisfied, fulfilled and certain that you are in the right place doing the right thing.

Assessment: For this particular application assessment is a multi-faceted step. You will work through the five-step process several times before you gain resolution around the issues that drove you to examine this partnership in the first place. Compare this partnership against the definition of partnership provided at the beginning of the application.

- Are you treated as an equal?
- Do you believe your partner to be your equal?
- Are you both independent of each other and yet have a moral and/or legal obligation to each other?
- Does each of you understand your obligations to this partnership in the same way?
- Is the weight of the partnership equal?
- Do you contribute equal resource, effort and emotional support to the partnership? If there is inequality, do you see it the same way and

189

have you both agreed to that unequal distribution of resource?

- Is one of you taking unfair advantage of the other? Has this been discussed and agreed to or simply assumed?
- Are you able to discuss the parts of the relationship that may feel skewed?
- Are you treated respectfully in the process?
- Do you treat the other person respectfully?
- If there is an unequal distribution of energy, resource and emotion, and it has not been agreed to, what is holding the partnership in place? Is it fear?
- Identify the fears which may be causing you to stay in a partnership which is not serving you. If you are taking advantage of the relationship at the other person's expense, identify the fears that may be holding your partner in place.

Engagement: Decide if this partnership is in sync with your vision. If it is not, decide to do something about it. Naturally, the first step is to realign the energy or resources in conjunction with your partner. Decide to discuss (clarity) the discrepancies, create a joint vision for continuation and attempt to execute that vision together.

Execute: After you have agreed to an intervention with your partner, monitor the result for consistency and adherence to the plan.

Outcomes:

What Should Happen: When both partners are committed to excellence in the relationship, you should be able to talk through inequities and agree together how to handle them. There should be an easy flow created out of your heightened awareness and joint commitment to excellence.

What Can Go Wrong: You may be too needy or dependent to demand or expect equality in your partnership. If so, you are a slave to the whims of the other person. Or, you may be in the opposite situation where you are the one taking advantage of the other person's neediness because you

need to have someone dependent on you to feel secure. Either situation is lacking in Grace.

How to Fix It: There is no easy fix for a partnership where the inequalities of the relationship create an inequity in satisfaction. You have the option of holding your ground in order to equal the playing field. If you do so, you must accept the risk that the relationship or partnership will dissolve if you do not succeed in getting the other person or people to own their responsibility to the partnership.

Advanced Intelligence:

True partnerships take enormous trust. You must trust the person to mean what he or she says. You must trust his or her intentions even when the behaviors are confusing. And, you must trust yourself enough to take on the risk of partnership. That means you could possibly lose. Do you trust the Universe enough to believe that if this partnership does not work, you will be ok? If you are afraid that you cannot exist without your partner, then you are in an unequal and potentially debilitating relationship. You will sacrifice Grace if you try to stay in a situation that may not be meeting your needs at all. Your dependence creates an unequal partnering which should not be good enough for a person of Confidence, Clarity and Trust.

Some Issues and Solutions:

Issue	Belief/Cause	Path to Grace
Your partner constantly overrides or discounts your needs and opinions.	Your partner believes that he or she is smarter, savvier and more sophisticated than you are. Therefore he or she is ordained to make decisions for you.	Get clear about how important the issue is to your well-being. Determine what you will do if there is no sense of collaboration around the issues on the part of your partner.

Your partner uses your commitment to the relationship to manipulate you to do things you do not want to do.	You believe that you signed on for better or worse and therefore you must acquiesce to your partner's demands even when they feel wrong or unfair.	Once again, seek clarity on what this partnership is supposed to mean for you as well as your partner. Review your understanding of the commitment with the other person and reach agreement. This does not mean agree with them if you do not feel that it is right. It means, reach agreement. Agreement may mean it is time to cut bait.
Your partner allows you to do anything you choose in the relationship because they are so needy that fear of you leaving the partnership holds them hostage.	You believe that it is ok for you to direct the flow of events affecting both of you because you are the savvier person in the relationship.	You must decide if this relationship feeds your soul. Are you in a real partnership or something else? Is that ok with you? Do you want to be in an unequal relationship? Do you find yourself moving the boundaries of the partnership because you seek more stimulation than that provided by your partner? Are you acting within the values you believe you stand for?

Application #19

Level I

Seeing the Macro

One of the most natural human responses is to view one's responsibility in terms of turf. You have established a perimeter or boundary and everything within that boundary is under your jurisdiction, command or responsibility. You hold yourself accountable to respond to any threat to that boundary or turf.

As you evolve your understanding of Grace, one of the challenges you must face is that you have a responsibility, not just to your immediate concerns, but to the entire ecosystem. Even if you execute flawlessly within your own parameters, until you feel a connection and responsibility to the larger whole, you are operating at sub-optimal performance.

As you grow, your understanding of the ecosystem grows as well. It is partially for this reason that the challenges of mastering Grace never end. If you are diligent and demanding enough to master Grace within your family, work environment and community you will find you need to stretch your horizon again to include an ever expanding ecosystem.

Objective:

- To develop and broaden your sense of responsibility to a larger and larger ecosystem.
- To build so much trust in the flow of the Universe that you are willing to see yourself responsible for a much greater arena than you would normally accept.

Prepare:

Define Your Initiative: Choose a professional or personal setting to explore. Define the boundaries of responsibility within that setting. In the situation you choose to explore, you are going to imagine that you are at least one,

193

possibly two levels up in the chain of command, and then identify how your view of reality would change as a result. If you choose your family, you will need to imagine that you are not only responsible for your family, but also for the larger community. This is difficult because many feel that the family is an indisputable boundary. People of Grace enlarge that perimeter to include the larger ecosystem. This view will definitely change your perspective in terms of handling problems.

Write a brief description of what you will work on in your journal!

The Challenge: Your immediate rewards may not be met and you could tighten up. As a result, you discontinue your sense of a larger arena. If you lose your nerve, you might fall back into expected behavior and the same old result of protecting your immediate turf. The consequence will be to flow. When a person loses the larger perspective, decisions will come in conflict with things that fall outside of that person's control.

The Skill Set: You will want to take your expanded sense of responsibility and help others cope with sacrificing their short-term wants and needs. This is an act of leadership and to be successful you will need to already have or gain their trust.

Approach:

You are attempting to define how your actions would change if you possessed, all of a sudden, a broader set of responsibilities.

Examine the five-step process:

Critical Moment: This becomes a critical moment, not necessarily because you are feeling angst but because you have an obligation to keep the larger ecosystem healthy even as you meet your former responsibilities. How willing are you to fight for important initiatives or ideas even if they do not affect your immediate concerns? For example, would you be willing to give up head count, if someone had a better idea than you do? Can you give up your ego enough to support what is important, or will you follow your knee-jerk response to get your share?

Vision: Enlarge your vision of success to include the entire entity, however you define it. It might be the family, the neighborhood, the company, the country etc. Let go of your fantasy of personal reward and recognition and imagine a healthy, vibrant whole, where you and your peers celebrate all successes equally. Imagine being willing to give whatever it takes to keep the whole healthy, even if it means sacrificing immediate reward or victory.

Assessment: Be clear on what would hold you back from doing so. Identify what you fear and what you would want to hold on to. Look carefully at both long-term and short-term risks for all your options. For example, there is a short-term risk in giving some of your control or rewards to someone with a great idea because it might not leave 'enough' for your own initiatives. Weigh this against the long-term risk to the whole of not realizing a great idea.

Engagement: Challenge yourself to embrace the short-term risks in favor of long-term ecosystem health. Make a decision to struggle more in the short-term if it means creating a solid base for the long-term.

Execution: Be sure to continue to assess the result as you embrace short-term risk and contribute your resources to the ecosystem. How does it feel? How do others respond? What happens to your options as a result?

Outcomes:

What Should Happen: You should find that by prioritizing what is important, others will respect you more rather than less, resources will increase rather than diminish and your ability to manage at higher levels will improve. You will be viewed as high potential and existing decision-makers will recognize that you think the way they think.

What Can Go Wrong: You may give up short-term results for long-term well being. Others may not appreciate your reasons, your subordinates may feel that you have sold them out and many may think that you are doing it for self-serving purposes.

How to Fix It: Check your intentions to make sure you are acting for the right reasons. You may have to trust the Universe and be patient for the result. You may not get an immediate return on your investment, but you will get the immediate satisfaction of doing the right thing for the right reasons. Ultimately, cause and effect will work in your favor. You must be prepared for that to take some time.

Advanced Intelligence:

There are always enough resources to do what is important. You live in an abundant Universe and there is always more than enough to go around.

Some issues and resolutions:

Issue	Cause/Belief	Path to Grace
One of your peers has a fabulous new product idea. It is your job to develop the product but you know it is outside your team's skill set. You do not want to admit you can't do it and you take on development, ending up with a watered down version of the design.	You are afraid that if you admit the project is beyond your team's skill set, the organization will lose confidence in you and your abilities.	Take the risk. Admit the truth and offer to help your peer find and fund the right resource. You are very likely to earn more respect rather than realizing your fear of being diminished. You are more than likely to be diminished if you ruin the product.

You are quite clever at the budgeting process. You recognize that if you ask for more than what you need you will have a safety net if your current projections are inaccurate.	You may believe that your action is justified. Everyone is doing it, and after all, if you do not, you'll end up looking foolish. Doing the right thing is hardly designed to make you look like a hero.	There are only so many resources to go around. Are you sure you should have all you're asking for? Are you afraid you won't be able to manage your business effectively if you don't have them? Ask yourself if you have the confidence to take the risk, or whether you are participating in a game that causes the organization to be less than effective.
You are on a well system for your water. Your neighbor's well is shallower than yours and during a long dry spell, their well runs dry. Do you tell them that you still have water? Do you share?	If they overtax your well, then you too will be without water. You imagine the worst case of your family having to dig a deeper well, or move because there is no water.	You will have to dig deep inside of yourself, and trust that whatever happens would have happened anyway. In the act of sharing, you will start a chain of cause and effect that may ultimately be the very thing that ensures your family's well-being. Since you cannot know, you must decide how you will live your life.

Application #20

Level II

Abundance vs. Scarcity

The stakes keep rising. To maintain flow during difficult moments you must constantly examine and adjust beliefs that you've held for a long time. One of the more common beliefs challenging our ability to respond with Grace to critical moments is something we will call "scarcity". This belief, often hidden in the background, causes us to hoard or recoil when we must make decisions of generosity.

We are trained to believe that we live in a dangerous and miserly Universe. We believe that if we give away what we have there will not be enough left over to meet our current or future needs. This is a hard belief to dispel. There is way too much evidence that this is indeed a Universe of scarcity as opposed to abundance.

This application challenges you to choose to believe in abundance. There are no promises or certainties. Choosing to live with Grace is choosing to live with uncertainty.

Objective:

1. To live your life guided by the belief that we live in a Universe of abundance where what is shared or given away will always leave you with exactly what you need to meet your needs.
2. To let go of your fear of not having enough and allow yourself to experience how differently your life flows when you do.

Prepare:

Define Your Initiative: As you discover yourself and your hidden beliefs by working through the applications, you will discover your own, unique fear of scarcity. You may believe you will never have enough money, security, love, time, etc. You may be incredibly competitive, which can reflect a symptom of scarcity. For example, if you do not win, you believe you will lose something. Or, if someone else gets the recognition, you will be diminished.

Choose something to work on which you recognize as your personal pattern of scarcity. Look for something in your life accompanied by a life-long fear that you would not have enough. For example, whatever you choose to hoard may represent your fear of scarcity. Whatever you are afraid of doing without may be your particular demon. You may have many. Just choose one. You have a lifetime to work on the others.

Write a brief description of what you will work on in your journal!

The Challenge: The greatest challenge is controlling your thoughts and your fears instead of letting them control you.

The Skill Set: You must increase your ability to interpret life in order to believe in abundance. You must look for evidence that the Universe is full of abundance and refuse to believe evidence to the contrary. Assume that evidence of scarcity is about lessons for living life.

If you are observant, you will see that two people can have exactly the same life experience and one person will create abundance while the other creates scarcity. The reason for the difference in their experiences can be found in how they think and how they respond, rather than what is real in the Universe.

Approach:

Approach this problem, your problem, as if you have been wrong all along. Pretend that you are going to see life through a new lens. Think of someone who you perceive to have an abundance of something you do not.

Focus on someone who believes they have an abundance of whatever you feel you are lacking. Use that person as a model to help you change your beliefs about scarcity.

Examine the five-step process:

Critical Moment: When you know that you are afraid of not having enough, see if you can break the fear down. Identify what you are afraid will happen. See if you can imagine your worst case scenario. Has it actually happened to you? Did you survive it? Are you afraid you won't survive next time?

Did you know that Walt Disney went bankrupt seven times? I wonder how many of us would have had the courage and creativity to continue on with an optimism that created the World of Disney after such set backs. Your fear is what you will wrestle with in order to get to Grace. You may have to accept what you are afraid of as part of life.

Vision: Create a vision in which you have more of whatever you fear is scarce than you can ever possibly use. Imagine winning the lotto or find a buried treasure—whatever represents an abundance of what you feel certain is scarce.

Assessment: Think about how you are living your life. Are you living a life of dependence? Are you placing your security or abundance in the hands of someone else? Are you sure that you need to do so, or are you doing it because you do not want to be responsible for yourself? Is the price of fear worth it?

Look at how you are living your life and the choices you are making. Is your fear a symptom of something else? Is it an indication that you are allowing yourself to be a victim? A fear of scarcity is often related to a fear of living your life fully.

Engagement: Start small. If, during the assessment step, you discover that you have given up being responsible and have given others control over what you fear, make a decision to take some of that responsibility back.

Wherever you feel you have no control is likely to be a place where you also fear scarcity.

Execution: Practice abundance. Practice giving away what you do not feel you have to someone who is even more in need. Test yourself. Is your fear that you never get enough recognition? Try giving recognition away and see what happens. Do you end up with nothing? Practice giving away an item every time you buy one for yourself. If you buy a purse, give away a purse. If you buy a new chair, give away a chair. See if your Universe gets smaller when you give away something each time you acquire something else. Experience the reality of generosity by practicing it and watching what happens when you do.

As you get better at generosity, practice on bigger things. Can you take a job for less money when you know you will be happier? Can you believe that the money will work out if you make the right decisions? Can you decide not to scrap over money in the divorce when someone is trying to hurt you? Can you choose to spend your energy differently? These are real challenges in many of our lives. You must decide between living your life believing in abundance or spending your life believing in scarcity.

Outcomes:

What Should Happen: You should find that you are never diminished after giving. You are never less for having passed something on. You should find you trust more the more you practice a belief in abundance.

What Can Go Wrong: You can go through hard times and decide that life really is about scarcity. As a result, you may return to a fear-based response to life and continue to validate what you fear.

How to Fix It: Do not take hard times personally and do not choose to believe that the hard times are about scarcity. Instead, believe that the hard times are teaching you something. Learn what you are meant to learn and then move on so you do not experience the same hard times again.

Advanced Intelligence: We create what we believe. If you believe that there is always enough, it is more than probable that you will always have enough. Even when things do not go your way, you will respond by believing that the tide will turn. As a result, you will do more of the things that bring good things back to you, and less of the things that repel the good things from you.

Some issues and resolutions:

Issue	Cause/Belief	Path to Grace
You never feel that your contributions are appreciated enough.	You want others to validate you so that you can believe in yourself.	Practice accepting that you receive more than enough recognition. See if you have been missing something which should have been obvious to you.
You are often afraid that others are trying to cheat you. You have validated it frequently which makes you even jumpier.	You are afraid that if others cheat you, you will end up with nothing.	Recognize that even when others cheat you, you are always able to recreate what you have lost. Those who cheat do not believe that they can create abundance other than through cheating. Let that be their problem.
You are afraid that you will end up old and poor and at the mercy of people who do not care about you.	You are so busy worrying about money that you are not doing the things that will give you confidence that the people in your life will always be there for you.	Put your energy into your relationships instead of your fear. Give of yourself to others and trust that they will give back when you are in need. Pay attention to cause and effect and be there for those who are in the situation you fear.

Appendix

In Depth Description of the Intelligence Do Loop

I. Critical Moment:

- *What is it?* Any moment where your response to it has the potential to affect the quality of your life could be considered a critical moment. Generally, when you identify a symptom (emotional, physical, or behavioral) of a "fall from Grace, you may identify that moment as a critical moment. All moments are important, but this one has your attention.

- *What Should Happen:* You should be able to identify what you are feeling and why. You will want to determine the nature of the emotion (is it fear, anger, frustration, etc?) You will want to be specific about why this moment is bothering you.

- *Advanced Intelligence:* The student aspiring to mastery of understanding critical moments will learn to identify whether a reaction to a specific moment fits into a pattern of other critical moments he or she has experienced. You are able to identify this moment as a part of a larger life's lesson and are therefore able to take responsibility for its occurrence.

- *What Can Go Wrong:* The most common mistake with critical moments is to ignore them or simply not be aware of them. When a person misses the critical moment he or she has a tendency to respond emotionally to the event or trigger. If you do not recognize that you are in a pivotal moment, your inclination will be to respond to the feelings generated by the moment without evaluating both the cause of the feelings and your next steps. In which case, you respond as you have always responded and you get what you have always gotten. So many of us go from one critical moment to another, never realizing their importance and never understanding that the chaos in our lives was avoidable if we had only paid attention.

- *How to Fix it:* If you miss a reaction as a critical moment, you will eventually figure it out because the tension will increase until you pay attention. Whatever is wrong with the moment, will always escalate if you fail to respond appropriately. If you identify the moment as a critical moment, and you attempt to work through the rest of the steps of the cycle thoughtfully and carefully and you continue to feel uneasy, unhappy or whatever it was that you felt in the first place, then you probably need to go back to creating a better definition of this critical moment and what is really the essence of why you have had the response you have.

- *The Challenge:* There are two major challenges with this step. The first one is to note that you are in a critical moment before simply reacting to what is occurring around you. The second is to really understand your part in creating this particular reaction so that you will identify a solution that actually has a chance of creating a quality of flow in the result. Sometimes you can better understand your part by testing your instinctive reaction for where it is in the cycle. Example: knee-jerk reaction to someone attempting to undermine your plan is to step immediately to execution without determining a vision, assessing risk and then identifying the correct decision based on those two steps.
- *The Skill Set:* It takes a lot of clarity to identify the exact nature of a critical moment. To do so, you must be adept at understanding the feelings and patterns which trigger your fear. If you can identify a moment as "this is my fear of the unknown setting me off again", you will find the way through the next steps with much more ease. The problem can almost always be described as a lack of confidence, clarity or Grace.

II. Vision:

- *What is it:* Your vision is your imagined result for whatever moment has your attention. Ideally vision is an active process where you are imagining the most positive, optimal result that could possibly occur as a result of your decisions and actions and responses.

- *What Should Happen:* If you are skilled at creating the vision in this step of the cycle, you should end up with an outcome where everyone involved feels the effortless flow of the interaction and result.

- *Advanced Intelligence:* The more a person trusts in the appropriateness of all circumstance, the more he or she is able to blend that understanding into a meaningful and harmonious vision. The more you believe in Grace, the more you will stretch your vision to include the more spiritual aspects of the possibilities.

- *What Can Go Wrong:* The first and most important failure occurs when your process of imagining the outcome is not conscious. You may vision the "worst" that can happen as a natural unconscious process. If you are thinking of your own needs without evaluating correctly the needs of others, the victory will seem unsatisfying. If you are criticized and do not understand why, it is likely your vision was incomplete in terms of identifying and meeting the needs of others.

- *How to fix it:* Unfortunately you won't know it has gone wrong until you are in the later stages of the cycle. People will resist you, obstacles will be endless, sabotage is a possibility. When things start going wrong, it is always a good idea to go back and ask if you were careful in constructing your vision of the desired result. Did you spend enough time on the visioning stage? Did you ask others what their vision was? Did you agree, find the compromise or if there was disagreement, did you simply move on with finding clarity?

- *The Challenge:* The biggest challenge in working through the vision step is to be sure that the vision is large enough. It is very difficult not to let obligations get in the way of the visioning process. There is plenty of time to weigh in the obligations when you are in the assessment stage of the cycle.

- *Skill Set:* Defining your visions based on who you are, your essence, and your destiny is a delicate operation. Finessing your vision to a nitty-gritty outcome that reflects you and how you want to integrate this specific moment into your life's journey is the objective.

III. Assessment:

- *What is it:* This is the step in the cycle of five-steps in which you must study the situation and yourself. In this step of the cycle, you are analyzing your dilemma and your options and you are assessing the different risks involved. You have already identified your fears and you are comparing them against the real vs imagined risks.

- *What should happen:* Ideally, you should compare your options against your vision to determine which course of action has the greatest likelihood of achieving the desired result. You should work to isolate and manage your fears logically in order to open yourself to pursue the most effective solution. You should also become very clear in this step about where you may be lacking Clarity, Confidence, or Trust. In the process, you should become clear about where and why you do not yet have enough information to make a good decision and you should seek that information.

- *Advanced intelligence:* If, during assessment, you were to focus on your Clarity, Confidence and Trust, and do problem solving around those three elements of your response, you raise your odds significantly of simply having the most optimal solution suddenly become very apparent.

- *What Can Go Wrong:* The most common error in this step is to let your fears control your assessment. Rather than becoming clear on the correctness of your information, your deductions, and the causes of your risk aversion, you might let fear take over and create a knee-jerk response in you which will only make your situation more difficult.

- *How to Fix it:* Help yourself to gain clarity by studying your history and observing the complications which have occurred in the past when you had similar reactions. Challenge yourself to identify the cause and effect chain in your own behaviors and to overcome the fears in order to create a different response.

- *The Challenge:* One of the bigger challenges to doing this step effectively is to overcome a sense of urgency in response. Give yourself the time to do this step properly and do not be tempted to respond before you have stepped back and analyzed your options and your fears for their relevance to the vision.

- *Skill Set:* This step demands that you evolve your problem solving skills. You will want to discipline yourself to examine all of your options and their implications deliberately before being seduced into a reaction. You will also want to be very clear about your blind spots and weaknesses and use logic to overcome their devastating impact on your life.

IV. *Engagement:*

- *What is it:* In the engagement step, you actually choose from your options and make your decision about your next move. Sometimes this is done independently and at other times you may be dialoguing with others as you reach a conclusion.

- *What should happen:* Because you have taken the time to gather information and assess the situation carefully, you should be fairly clear about the correct decision. If others resist your conclusion in this stage, you should assume that you do not yet have enough information. This would cause you to go back to step III.

- *Advanced intelligence:* Making decisions about how to handle critical moments is a dynamic, flexible process. Like taking a sailboat into the wind, you should be ready to change quickly as more information becomes available and as you see the results of each move you make. When you are in the flow, you move quickly back and forth among all the steps as the results reveal the cause and effect nature of reality. In the stage of making the decision, the Ego can play a big role and your ability to balance your sense of superiority with your understanding of the needs and contributions of others may affect the quality of your outcome dramatically.

- *What Can Go Wrong:* If you make the wrong decision and do not pay attention to the signals you receive, you may be too fixated on things unfolding according to your plan.
- *How to Fix it:* Humility and constant vigilance are the cures to blindly pursuing the wrong path. Repeatedly putting yourself back into vision and assessment mode are your best choices when things go wrong.

- *The Challenge:* the EGO and a need to be right as opposed to a true desire to always operate from a state of Clarity, Confidence and Trust.

- *Skill Set:* Being alert to the nuances of the moment, feedback or resistance of others, and being able to overcome your own fears in order to change your mind are all important qualities and skills. Recognizing patterns in the moment is difficult and takes practice.

V. Execution

- *What is it?:* The stage of the cycle where the actions play into results. Commitments are kept or broken.

- *What should happen:* If you have done your diligence in the previous steps, you should find this step effortless and uneventful.

- *Advanced intelligence:* If you find yourself turning into a tank or becoming controlling in this step, it is highly likely that you have not yet recognized that you are not nor ever will be, in control. Such a realization often comes after great pain. Learning to recognize the perfection of the greater force is a highly advanced state.

- *? Everything.* This is the step in the cycle where you get feedback from the path itself. Every flaw in your thinking in working through the previous steps will become apparent in the result, but perhaps not in the cause. Things start to feel uncomfortable, jerky, off in some way.

- *How to Fix it:* Pay attention to how things flow and feel and when it is not the way it should be, go back and rework the steps again and again with small and large adjustments as needed.

- *The Challenge:* Life and your mastery of life is the real challenge. Each time you get symptoms of chaos, you are in charge of your response. If you choose to be victimized by what does not work, your frustration will grow. It will feel like being in a maze with no apparent way out. The challenge is to always assume responsibility for what is not working and find your own contribution to that truth.

- *Skill Set:* Recognizing your own symptoms of stress and fear are the most important skills to have in any stage of the process. When it goes wrong, do you move quickly to solutions or do you get stuck in your fears or your lack of Confidence?

Definitions

Clarity: Being able to see all aspects of an issue with a particular emphasis on how that issue ties into the laws of cause and effect.

Confidence: A trust in your own ability to identify and resolve issues before they take on the quality of a crisis.

Trust: An assumption that all things fall into a state of perfect synchronicity with everything you need to create flow and ease in your reality.

As you gain an understanding of trust, there is a short story that you can find in Carolyn Myss's book Sacred Contracts which really clarifies a Trust in the wisdom of the Universe. She is telling of a dream she had where she is an only passenger on a plane sitting on a runway. The other planes, one after another are cleared to take off while she sits. In anger, she wants to know why the control tower is not letting her go. The response is basically, "Turn off your motors. We are waiting until the skies are safe."

Grace: Connection to a state of Clarity, Confidence and Trust.

Super-Positioning: A state of heightened awareness attainable only when one has conquered the obstacles to Confidence, Clarity, and Trust. Super Positioning is that state in which a person has the ability to solve problems in a way which factors all variables and potential obstacles into the solution.

Do Loop: A state of disconnection from your higher levels of understanding, causing you to repeat the same errors and create the same uncomfortable outcomes.

Cause and Effect: A consistent and pervasive reality, which links all outcomes to a set of actions or behaviors.

Scarcity: A belief that in most situations, the worst case possibility is the likely outcome.

Partnering: Accepting that an individual is your equal. This person brings a richness to the outcome which must be respected and nurtured.

Bully: A person who lacks imagination and interactive skills, and therefore uses Bullying to achieve his or her agenda.

Hot Lava: The descriptor of the results which occur when one is in a state of Super-Positioning. Hot Lava is the ability to move toward your objectives as an unstoppable force which overcomes all resistance.

Fold em': A phrase often used in poker to indicate the moment when a person decides that he or she has carried the hand forward to the point where the outcome clearly indicates that there is no point in pressing forward. In the world of attaining Grace, fold em' is the moment when a person realizes that letting go is the only reasonable solution as all other paths lead to more of the same.

Some General Mistakes

1. Missing the critical moment when it first arrives.

2. Being ahead of yourself.
    a. Trying to make decisions when you do not have a clear vision.
    b. Trying to make decisions when you do not have all the facts.
    c. Being in execution mode when others have not agreed.
    d. Bullying others to agreement and finding they do not follow through because they never really agreed with you.

3. Failing to identify new critical moments within each of the steps.

4. Failing to be sure that the fundamentals of Confidence, Clarity and Trust are in place in each step before moving into the next steps.

5. Not respecting others' need to work through the cycle on any joint initiative.

6. Not understanding the symptoms of being in the wrong step of the cycle.

7. Not being clear about your most appropriate contribution. Not having a clear sense of who you are and how to apply it. Getting lost in trying to meet expectations of others rather than in setting and meeting expectations in yourself.

In Depth Case Study

You despise your boss because you believe he or she lacks integrity! You cannot stand to be in the same room with this person and find yourself highly offended when they are unhappy or critical of you. "How dare this person judge me, given how crude, base, out of control, he is?" might be a language that feels appropriate to you.

Finding Grace:

Step One: Critical Moment

1. Identify this as a critical moment. Make a list of any other past moments that felt or were similar in nature with this or other people.

2. Identify what you believe regarding his or her behavior. You might say, "I find this person to be arrogant and crude."

3. Clarity. Identify what you *feel* when you are exposed to this behavior. This is actually the most important step in the process and you will want to understand the subtleties of your feelings. For example, the first three listed here might be the ones that first come to mind, but fourth is more of the underlying feeling which causes the most intense part of your reaction..
    a. Offended
    b. Angry
    c. Disgusted
    d. Anxiety/fear

4. Confidence: Ask yourself if you are feeling totally self confident in this person's presence or if somehow this behavior sets off some sort of insecurity in you. Do you find yourself trying to get this person's

approval in spite of how you feel about him or her? Ask why if the answer is "yes"

5. Trust: Assume that this person is symbolic of something you need to work through. What would you have to believe that would make this a non issue for you?
   a. Everything is in perfect flow. I am reacting to this because I am not. If I am coming from judgment of his or her imperfections, it is costing *me*.
   b. I accept that he or she has his or her own lessons to learn and that I do not need to let them bother me as he or she works it through. I am not in charge of fixing this person!
   c. If I stop resisting this person's nature, it will be easier for me to work more effectively with or around her or him. I resist because I continually fall into the trap of trying to make the person see the error of his ways.

Step 2: Vision

1. Create a vision for the ideal resolution of this situation in terms of how it feels. Challenge yourself to come from confidence, Trust and clarity in terms of this vision, rather than insecurity and fear.

2. Your vision should accommodate the nature of the solution, not the solution. For example, wanting this person fired is a goal rather than a vision. Wanting a headhunter to contact you so that you can start a new job is also a goal rather than a vision, and in fact, practically assures that you will have more falls from Grace since you have not fixed you!

3. An example of an appropriate vision might be: I would like to be so clear about who I am and to be so comfortable within myself, that when I encounter people like my current boss in the future, they will not cause me to even miss a beat. I will flow around that person's idiosyncrasies with ease. I will understand that it is not my problem

and I will remove myself from the potential argument, understanding that it is not my job to make anyone else see his or her own flaws.

Step 3: Analysis or assessment

1. I will identify my options and become clear headed rather than emotional about my choices.

   a. I can continue on as I am. This includes holding onto all of my biases. This option contains the risk of continuing to feel angry and or fearful. If I do so, I will also continue to get the fallout of my own negative behavior. Others will find me difficult and I will get a reputation as such.

   b. I can allow this person to continue behaving as they are but I will not allow myself to react. The risk inherent in this choice is that I will be unable to let go of my intense feelings and I will fail at this.

   c. I can quit. The risk in this is that every time I encounter people with this personality, it will cause me to make life choices I do not want to make. I know this because of the list I made of this type of issue in Step 1.

   d. I can identify the good traits that my boss actually does have (*everyone* has good traits no matter how stuck you are in believing that this person is beyond redemption). I will focus on those traits, allow the rest to unfold, assume that it is unfolding as it should, and be peaceful about the way it is going.

Step 4: Engagement

- You look at your options along with your vision and decide to go for step d above. You determine that one of your boss's best traits is that he likes to "grow" people and particular likes the role of mentor. You decide to let his negative traits be his problem and his karma, and you make the decision that you will swallow your Pride and ask for him to teach you what he knows about the function that you are in.

- You also spend time identifying what it is about his behavior that triggers such an intense reaction in you. Why does his lack of integrity make you feel as though you want to punish him?
    - You are angry because he is hurting the organization
    - You are angry because the organization is letting him get away with it.
    - You are angry because you believe that his choices reflect on you.
    - You are angry because even when you explain quite rationally what you see, others do not understand or get it.
    - You seem to be getting blamed for what you are doing wrong and his behaviors are far worse.
    - You realize that you think that the world is being unfair to you and you resent that you suffer because of his inadequacies.

Step 5: Execution:

- You initiate a conversation with your boss asking for his help in learning what he expects, why he expects it and what he is looking for.

- You express curiosity (clarity) about what his experience in dealing with you has been.

- You watch for critical moments in your own responses to find when you have fallen back into judging this person and therefore back into your own sense of angst.

- You become his ally and a loyal subordinate without trying to change him. You act on your decision to allow the Universe and others to show him what he has yet to learn. You are too consumed managing your own responses to worry about what is wrong with him.

5.   You realize that the organization is an entity. If it were totally healthy, it would reject his behavior. Perhaps waiting for the organization to mature enough to deal with his behavior is a more appropriate response.

What you can expect:

- You are now set up to be more successful with this individual. By stepping out of the way by letting go of trying to fix him, it is highly likely that others in the organization will see his behavior more clearly and will act on what is wrong. Often these people are then held more accountable for their actions. Before, everyone was just trying to stay out of the way of both of you and the intensity of your interaction.

- You will feel mellower towards this person and he will relax some of his need to control your responses as well.

- You will begin to enjoy the relationship in spite of everything you are feeling right now.

- You have had these feelings for a long time. It is probable that you will once again fall into anger or dislike. If you have any kind of emotional reaction, assume that it is a critical moment and identify what it is about this moment that you are reacting to.

- Your boss does not respond positively to your request for mentoring (highly unlikely).

- Your boss continues to move up the food chain as if rewarded for his bad behavior.

More About Trust

Try to imagine yourself in the following situation and feel what you must feel.

You find you're starting to lose vision in right eye. Your ophthalmologist does not find anything and suggests perhaps you have an irritation of the optic nerve. Relieved, you even now continue to push for clarity and visit next with a specialist who orders an MRI just to be cautious.

The next morning you immediately scheduled for a biopsy on the shadow behind your eye that appeared in the MRI. Within days you will be experiencing chemotherapy for the first time, with a preliminary diagnosis of Lymphoma.

The gauntlet begins. You are now separate from everyone else who does not have cancer. You will never see life in the same way as you did just days ago. You will never be the same.

You start with needing to know everything you can about the disease. Lymphoma is fast growing so while that sounds like the bad news, it is treatable by chemo, which attacks fast growing cells. You are again relieved. You think, "I can get through this."

The next journey is to pick your doctor, which is in effect, picking your treatment. This all needs to be done extremely quickly. They all seem to do it a little differently and they articulate very good reasons for their choices. How will you know? You are not an expert. How quickly can you become one? How quickly can you choose one? This is a fast moving train with little time for reflection!

You ask the questions and you arrive at the door of the "expert". He is curious and wants to know more about your special (rare) form of this disease. You are intense about wanting to get started with fighting this invasion, and yet, he says, "Let's wait a week. I want to see more from pathology. I am not sure that this is lymphoma. It could be one of two other kinds of cancer, both of them very bad."

You want your lymphoma back. It now seems as if life was simple when it was just lymphoma.

You just got clear on the enemy and you are ready to fight, *now.* "More research" gives your control to someone else again and you feel like a victim. A *week.* An eternity!

Do you have the dreaded option #1 which gives you a 50% chance of being alive in the next 2 years, or option #2, which offers the dimmer 10% view? You get through the week by talking to friends and exploring your sense of you. How did you get this disease? It was never going to be you. It was other people for whom you had empathy, but you live a healthy life and take care of yourself. Who *are* you now that you have CANCER?

The week of waiting is over. You are different, but you are still you. You are in a funny place when you arrive to hear what it is that you have inside of you. You know that no matter what happens, you are going to hear bad news. And yet, none of this seems real. It is as if someone else is this new person who has cancer.

As you numbly listen to the result (#2), you wonder if you heard the doctor correctly. You have a rare form of cancer that gives you a less than 10% chance of being alive in two years (sinonasal undifferentiated carcinoma, SNUC). By now, you are becoming familiar with bad news and this is just another level of the nightmare unfolding over the last two weeks. Could life really be that different in just two weeks? Interestingly, when they announce the survival rate, you KNOW that it has no additional impact on your thinking or your ability to overcome the odds.

But, your life is different. At this point you might think that the system should just take over. You want to just go inside and deal with this new you, but the decisions you must now make about who will treat you and in what way are crucial. You drag yourself through the process of deciding, and treatment finally begins. You are very glad you stayed present because you found that some of the options presented to you were not what they seemed and needed to be discarded. Woe unto the person who simply trusted the information he or she was given.

You are to have two kinds of treatment since the tumor is inoperable. You will blast this intruder with both chemicals and radiation and you begin to understand what that will mean to your body. You start the process, and somehow it isn't as bad as you thought it would be.

But here is where you make your biggest decision. Who will you be in this new understanding of your journey? Will you be like all of the other victims you watch marching to their treatments with so much fear in their eyes? Will you give control to this invader? Or should you give yourself over to those who push the victims through the system on the cancer conveyor belt?

Breathe! After all, this is not really you.

It is however, a true story. And the person in this story made an important decision as he entered into this face-off with death. He decided he was still alive.

He decided to trust. Trust what? A faith in God? A faith in himself? A faith in modern medicine? All of the above and none of the above. He decided to just totally Trust that he had control over his own fate.

He explored the outcome of his own death, and he was not frightened. He explored the option of living and he was not frightened. It would be what it would be, but his decision was about *how* he would go through the process and *what* he would believe as he did.

He chose to think of himself as someone who had been invaded by a very bad entity; not as a victim of a bad disease, but as someone who had been wronged. He attacked the disease as one might attack an intruder with a knife, not with fear but with outrage. He trusted the system, but only as far as was prudent. After all, this was *his* life and he was still in charge. He decided that he deserved to be treated well by the system and he was deserving of victory.

He began to consciously think of himself as worthy of good health and daily/repeatedly said out loud with conviction, "I am a healthy and cancer free person!" He decided to fight with a positive spirit and humor.

"Bring it on," he would say as they hooked him up. "I am paying for this, so make sure I get my full share."

At three months, *before* the treatments were complete, he was told that there was "no evidence of disease" by a gaggle of doctors who were mystified.

He celebrated like a conqueror. He knew that the battle might come again. He was not foolish. But he would fight the next battle if and when it came. Not today and not tomorrow. Why give his life energy to an enemy who had already been defeated? He would fight it *if* it came again. By making this choice, he was again choosing not to let fear rule the quality of his life. It was *his* life, not the cancer's, not the doctors', and not the chemo's and radiation's. No one and nothing else owned the outcome and no one else would live with the consequences of his choices. He ruled his life and trusted in his ability to simply say "NO" to the cancer.

Each of us will at sometime be faced with, or participate in, crisis. Some crises, like facing cancer, are uniquely personal. Regardless of those who were touched by this man's situation, the battle was between him, his attacker and his beliefs. While the choice of doctors and treatments is extremely relevant, at some point, he had to find his stance within the bombarding emotions which come with the crisis. He chose to approach this situation with Confidence in his own right to live, with Clarity about the nature of the enemy, the cure, and the healers, and with Trust in his own ability to choose.